Our Creative Fingerprint

Our Creative Fingerprint

Nancy Carter Pennington, M.S.W.

Lawrence H. Staples, Ph.D.

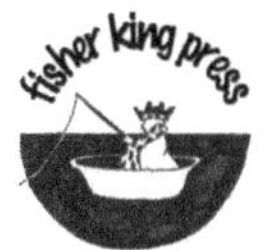

CONTENTS

Acknowledgments vii

Authors' Note viii

I. Creativity and Inner Truth 1

II. Divine Discontent: The Inner Urge to Create 23

III. Transformation: Cleaning Our Psychic Augean Stables 47

IV. Creativity and Rebirth 67

Afterword 75

Bibliography 76

Index 78

ACKNOWLEDGMENTS

We wish to thank all the men and women who over many years have shared with us their creative gifts, their artistic productions, and their experiences of and insights into the creative process. In order to protect their privacy and confidentiality, where we have used case material, we have used fictionalized composites.

This is the fourth book Fisher King Press has published for us. These books simply could not have come to life without the enduring support, encouragement, and counsel of Mel Mathews, the publisher of Fisher King Press. In previous books we have already alluded to Mel's vision, patience, and sheer brilliance. He is also an accomplished writer who has contributed meaningfully to the preparation and development of our manuscripts. Again, Mel, thanks from the bottoms of our hearts.

Our editor, Karen Farley, brought to our manuscript not only her incredible technical skills and her amazing gift with words, but also a deep and sophisticated knowledge of Jungian psychology. What was most remarkable to us was her ability not only to edit beautifully but to do it in a way so seamless that it never impaired or lost the voice or soul of our work. In our experience, this is a rare gift, indeed. She also has a remarkable work ethic whose presence was reflected in her high levels of productivity and responsiveness. Thanks, Karen. It was a great pleasure to work with you.

A special thanks also goes to Peter V. Emerson, whose amazing creative gifts helped us revise, adapt, and develop Part II of *Our Creative Fingerprint* into a blog post entitled, "Unhappiness: The Agent of Change," that appeared in *The Huffington Post* in 2016.

AUTHORS' NOTE

This book grew from a chapter we had written for an anthology about creativity. We aborted that work before it was finished but sent a draft of the intended chapter to our friend, Peter Emerson. He liked the piece and felt it could be made into an excellent blog post for *The Huffington Post* if we made it shorter and somewhat more mainstream in flavor. With Peter's remarkable creative help, the piece appeared in the April 20, 2016, *Huffington Post* under the title, "Unhappiness: The Agent of Change."

The initial piece, from which this book grew, now appears as Part II of *Our Creative Fingerprint*. While Part II contains significant new material, it also retains much of the original piece as well as *The Huffington Post* blog post adapted from it.

Our Creative Fingerprint is not an academic or scholarly work, but we have acknowledged sources that we have quoted or drawn upon with footnotes.

This above all: to thine own self be true,
And it must follow, as the night the day,
Thou canst not then be false to any man.
—William Shakespeare

I

CREATIVITY AND INNER TRUTH

We are never more true to ourselves than when we are creating something. Our creations have an inescapable integrity. Inexorably, they reflect our selves[1] as profoundly, as faithfully, and as uniquely as our fingerprints, which, like our inner selves, were there in the beginning. We all, not just Picasso or Einstein or Beethoven or Frank Lloyd Wright, have a unique identity that, like fingerprints, we project onto all our creative work. People who study art, music, literature, or architecture can identify the painter's, composer's, author's, or architect's work without seeing a signature. They know that a painting was by Caravaggio or Manet, or that a piece of music was written by Stravinsky or Wagner, or a book by Hemingway, or that a building was designed by Louis Kahn or Frank Lloyd Wright. Without actually having encountered a piece before, they know whose it is by inference and intuition applied to a host of artistic nuances like cadence, tone, style, word usage and sequences, contrast, color, light, composition, brushstroke, and other tell-tale subtleties.

Our physical self is relatively easy to see. We have readily available conventional mirrors that permit us to see our physical selves. There is always something visibly unique that helps identify us. For example, the parents and siblings of twins can usually tell them apart. It is far more difficult to "see" our psychic selves. There are no psychic mirrors

---

1 Throughout this volume, we use the word "ourselves" to refer to the standard definition of the term, that is, "we, us, the physical person," and two words, "our selves" to refer to the inner person, the self as a psychic entity or psychological or philosophical concept.

readily available to us, unless we had exceptional parents who could fully, without harsh judgment, reflect our selves back to us. The problem is that such a parent exists only in theory. Real parents cannot mirror us accurately because they project themselves onto us and so see themselves more than they see us. Fortunately, what we create is, perhaps, the most complete and particular manifestation of our psychic selves. Thus, in the absence of such an ideal parent, creative work serves as a surrogate parent that reflects us back more accurately and helps us discover and see our selves more completely than any real parent can.

Over time our collective works reveal more and more of our selves. Still, each single thing we create, no matter when or under what conditions it was produced, will bear trace deposits of our selves sufficient to identify us and show who we are. Our actual fingerprints are similarly unerring to those who know enough to interpret them. Just as ten fingerprints will reveal more of our identity than a single fingerprint, one is sufficient to know who we are. We cannot escape our selves no matter how much consciously we may try to hide. In all art there is an underlying voice that cannot be completely hidden or extinguished. In the long run, forgeries will be detected.

In the end, all of our creations are self-portraits. We see our selves in them. One way to understand this process of self-portraiture is to observe an impressionist painting of, say, a landscape. Compare the painting with a photograph of the same landscape. What is the difference between the two? The difference is the artist, and that difference reflects both conscious and unconscious contents supplied by the artist. Where the painting resembles the photo, we see more conscious contents of the artist; where the painting resembles something less known to us, it reflects the images normally not readily available to the artist's conscious mind.

It is this very tendency of our creations to faithfully mirror our selves that may explain why, at some deep level, our creations repeat themselves in ever-recurring leitmotifs that run indelibly, *roten faden*, through all our work. We repeat because our creative work can reflect only one thing, our selves. For each individual, this is a single, unique self. Ultimately, our art can only reflect our self and the particular issues, themes, and complexes that are important to it. It's not interested in someone else's story and so exerts enormous pressure to hold us to its own narrative. We can only manifest the particular "I am" that we are. Thus, if our work is to be true to our selves, we must insistently repeat ourselves. And it will follow as unremittingly "as the night the day" that in so doing we "canst not then be false to any man." When we create, our work always expresses our self just as an oak always expresses itself in its acorn. The acorn is to the oak as our art is to our self, and our art can no more be false to our self than an acorn can be false to its oak and develop into some other type of tree. Carl Jung, the Swiss psychiatrist, has used the phrase, "the inability to do otherwise"[2] to describe this phenomenon. Or, as Jung has also said, in the end, we remain obstinately ourselves until all sides of our reality are recognized.[3]

Artists are often aware of some underlying force that, like a powerful undertow, draws them tenaciously to a central story, despite conscious wishes they may have to do otherwise. Some can give voice to this phenomenon. Speaking at a news conference after winning the 2014 Nobel Prize in Literature, Patrick Modiano, the French writer, described succinctly this tendency in himself: "I have always felt like I've been writing the same book for the past 45 years." His words remind us of a conversation we had in Florence in 1998 at the 14th Congress for Analytical Psychology. We were speaking with a colleague when he asked us if we knew how many symphonies Vivaldi had written. Of course, we replied, "No." He smiled and said, "Four hundred, the same one four hundred times." Similarly, in a well-known Swedish TV series, we see the middle-aged son of an artist asking his father why he always paints the same thing. The father replies that each day when he gets up he has the intention of painting something else, "a still life, maybe an abstract, just splash the paint, see where it takes me. And then I start, and every time, I paint the same thing. The landscape."[4]

The proclivity of artists to repeat themselves is also portrayed humorously in a story about Winslow Homer, a famous American seascape

---

2 C.G. Jung, 1969. "The Psychology of the Child Archetype," CW 9i, ¶ 289.
3 C.G. Jung, 1967. "The Problem of the Attitude Type," CW 7, ¶ 93.
4 *Wallander*, "Sidetracked," directed by Philip Martin (2008; London, UK: BBC Video, 2009), DVD.

painter. A wealthy American reportedly asked Homer to paint his portrait. Homer refused, saying he only painted seascapes. The wealthy man persisted and finally offered Homer $5 million to paint his portrait. As the story goes, Homer consented, but told his patron not to be surprised if, when completed, the painting looked like a seascape!

Some might observe recurrent patterns in creative production of an artist and be critical, as in the comment about Vivaldi. They may interpret it as some kind of loss of creative inspiration or as a kind of creative laziness. They may see the tendency to repeat as pejorative; we see it as, perhaps, the supreme compliment. Because our creations reflect and mirror our selves, creative work that permits us to see and express our selves again and again from widely differing angles and perspectives is essential both to self-discovery and to the deep and richly meaningful art that flows from it. This may be why Cézanne would paint the same landscape at varying times and on different days or why Frida Kahlo painted numerous self-portraits. While all artists may not always be consciously aware of the self-discovery purpose of their works, as psychologists, we know this to be a powerful motivating urge.

Repetition itself is a powerful catalyst that helps open the door to the unconscious reservoir of the yet-undiscovered parts of our selves that want to be seen and expressed. It works its door-opening magic in a way that bears much similarity to the process of meditation. When we meditate, we may repeat a word or breathe repeatedly in and out. Eventually, this repetition carries us to a transcendent place that yoga masters refer to as "transcending." Runners can have a similar experience. The repeated footfalls lead to an experience of the unconscious that is not unlike meditation. Runners enter what they sometimes refer to as "the zone." We have read that when Alfred, Lord Tennyson wanted to write a poem, he would put himself in a mystic trance by repeating his own name.[5] Repetition leads us to a deep part of our selves, just as dreams do when we are asleep and the ego is weakened. The repetition somehow temporarily diminishes or disables the ego and opens doors

---

5 John van Druten, *I Am A Camera: A Play in Three Acts* (New York: Dramatists Play Service, 1983), 10, http://www.worldcat.org/title/i-am-a-camera-a-play-in-three-acts/oclc/879155434/viewport.

to some space that lies outside ego consciousness. Perhaps that is why psychiatrists have been called "shrinks." Today, therapists of many types can help patients shrink their egos sufficiently to open, at least for brief periods, a door that has stood in the way of complete self-development. Bypassing the ego thus enables them to discover and integrate qualities that are needed to understand themselves and their problems and to live life more fully. The simple process of doing creative work opens to varying degrees the door to the unconscious and leads us to our self. And it makes no difference whether the creative work is deemed good or artistic by any standards.

Clearly, sufficient repetition can shift control away from the ego's will and intention and cause it, at least temporarily, to operate like the autonomic nervous system. Our breathing and many of our most important bodily functions operate this way, without will or intention on the part of the ego. Because the ego is out of the loop, things operate more naturally and efficiently. A basketball player repeats shots again and again and again. Eventually, he doesn't think about them. Until he reaches this point, the ball goes to the left or right or falls short. Similarly, we like to go to surgeons who have done an operation many times. They too become proficient from repetition. The ego has a tendency to be one-sided, to prefer one of the opposites over another. And when the ego is too strong and present, we are one-sided. Then, when we shoot basketballs or throw footballs or make an incision, or write words or compose notes or make brushstrokes, we may miss the mark.

Many artists, like meditators or runners, have the experience of getting into a "zone." Instead of pounding the pavement, they are pounding the keyboard or stroking the canvas. It's hard work. It's a struggle. But they keep doing the same thing again and again, word after word, stroke after stroke. Suddenly, something kicks in. They're in the zone and the writing or painting flows. Suddenly, they feel as if they have just tapped a hidden spring from which a torrent of words, notes, or images pours forth.

One can sense intuitively that these outpourings bear at least some metaphorical relationship to the huge production of energy that occurs in the chain reaction that begins with the splitting of a single atom.

Metaphorically, at least, chemical compounds begin with the smallest elemental particles, just as a book begins with an elemental particle we call "a word." Electromagnetic attraction of oppositely charged sub-atomic particles leads to the bonding of smaller elements which combine to create larger ones. While the process of creation in the literary field cannot be demonstrated in the same way as chemical changes, Jung and Freud's work with association suggests that words also are elemental particles that can bond together in particular ways to form larger entities. It is as if there is a "word magnet" in an author's psyche—or a "color and form magnet" inside a painter's—that draws together into a creative opus the particular words or images that must be bound in close association if a particular work is to be produced. While it is impossible to directly compare the processes underlying the creation of chemical and literary compounds, it feels at an intuitive level as if the processes do indeed resemble each other in certain ways.

The freer, less-fettered flow that occurs when the ego is not fully in charge leads us to think that repetition's ego-weakening tendency reduces the tension and, therefore, the resistance between the ego and the unconscious, permitting them to come into alignment. It causes "at-one-ment." The conscious and the unconscious behave, at least in the creative moment when we are in that "zone," as if they are one. The opposites merge, and we get artistically pregnant and produce a third, our work, the child of our creative intercourse.

Creative work is the handmaiden of self-discovery. It leads us to our self. It leads us home to the place where we started, so that we can connect with our self, know it, and express it. No matter where our creative work starts or what path it follows—with a word, with a note, with a brushstroke—it eventually, with repeated effort, takes us home and connects us to our self, which informs and infuses our work with itself and returns it to a page or a canvas or a score. The idea that creative work leads us to and connects us to our self is captured in the following poem written by one of our patients:

All Roads Lead to Rome

What does it mean to say

That all roads lead to Rome?
It's a mystery in a way,
Like writing a simple poem.
Like conversations with old friends,
From any theme departed,
Lead relentless toward those ends
We knew before we started.
A process known by Jung and Freud,
Start with any word.
A chain reaction fills the void,
Brilliant and absurd.
Control is lost; will is broken.
Something very deep takes over
Once the magic word is spoken,
Searches for the four-leaf clover.
Jazz pianists also know,
The first note they can choose.
All the other notes just go
Like feelings fired by booze.
Directed by some unseen hand,
Notes and feelings gonging,
The great conductor of the band
Knows their secret longing.
No matter where we seem to be,
However far we roam,
Some super magnet we can't see
Will always lead us home.
And like the song the cynic wrote
To ridicule our Rome:
"Be it ever so decadent,
There's no place like home."[6]

---

6 Used by permission. The last two lines appear to be taken from a song
  written by Tom Lehrer, a college math teacher who also was a songwriter
  and entertainer.

In any event, a pretty good case can be made for some kind of "unconscious knowingness" being embedded in the creative process. It knows what things belong together in order to create the work. Since the work is a reflection of our selves, it also knows what things go together to create our selves. It will put us on roads that seem to go in different directions but always take us to Rome. They take us home. They lead us to our "I am."

Repetitive creative work can lead not only to far-reaching self-discovery, but also to the great art that is infused with it. A dramatic example of this can be seen in the paintings of Frida Kahlo.[7] Frida was raised by parents who could not have been more opposite. Her mother was Mexican, rigidly Catholic, cool, and puritanical. Her mother had grown up in an age when Mexican women were not allowed to say the word "buttocks"; rather, they would say "that which I sit on." Nor could they say the word "legs"; rather, "that which I stand on." And, as in the movie *Like Water for Chocolate*,[8] they were not allowed to look at their bodies. They were taught to feel guilt and shame about their bodies and themselves. Much of what we would call normal life today was cut off from them. Frida's mother was severe and frowned on much of what Frida did and who she was.

Frida's father was a Jew who had immigrated from Germany. He had a completely different cultural and religious experience from her mother. Many accounts report him to have been overly solicitous of and close to Frida, especially after she hurt her foot when she was nine years old. All the children in her family were girls, and she became her father's favorite and tried to be the boy he yearned for but never had. She was torn by the wholly different views and values of her parents but behaved in ways that were more acceptable to her father. She was every bit the tomboy, but she was also a lively and mischievous young girl. In her life, she was very unconventional when compared to traditional Mexican women at the time. She drank, smoked, was bisexual, and had

---

7 Some background information and facts were drawn from the brilliant work of art historian Helga Prignitz-Poda in her book, *Frida Kahlo: The Painter and Her Work* (Munich: Schirmer/Mosel Publishers, 2004).

8 *Like Water for Chocolate*, directed by Alfonso Arau (1993; Santa Monica, CA: Miramax Lionsgate, 2000), DVD.

several abortions, and she was assertive and successful in a chosen career in which she distinguished herself.

At the age of sixteen, Frida nearly died in a terrible accident, breaking her vertebrae in three places, along with her leg, foot, shoulder, and ribs. She was left partially crippled. After she recovered, she began to paint. It was as if her paintings were a collage on which she was pasting herself back together. Her paintings were mostly self-portraits. She could literally see herself in her paintings, her mirrors. She was fascinated with her body, which her mother had disallowed. While she was recuperating, she had had a mirror installed over her bed. Some instinct led her to sense the deep need for mirroring that she had not received as a child. Raised with such rigid, conflicting worldviews and values, she was cut off from parts of herself, and her painting was an attempt to create her own mirror so that she could restore herself. The accident Frida had at age sixteen profoundly affected her life and her ability to live it fully. Her painting was essentially her autobiography.

On the following pages, we would like to show and discuss some of Frida Kahlo's paintings. Frida produced only 143 known paintings, but these, nevertheless, led to world renown. There is, unfortunately, time only for a superficial trip through a few paintings of deep beauty and profound meaning. Here, we will simply try to call to your attention some aspects of her art, mirrored by her paintings, that suggest a divided and fragmented self that is groping toward a yearned-for wholeness.

The first painting (Figure 1 on page 11) is called *What I Saw in the Water*. If this were a dream or fairy tale, we would likely speculate that we are looking here at unconscious contents that reveal a wounded, fragmented, and divided self. The disparate contents appear to have little coherence. In the foreground, we see an empty dress. Art historian and author Helga Prignitz-Poda notes:

> This is a traditional, Tehuana dress worn by women in the Tehuantepec region of Mexico. While the men in this region tend to be more domestic, the women to the present day dominate the commercial and social life in the market place and in the bars. It is one of the few regions in the world where the matriarchy is preserved. This dress became a kind of hallmark for Frida.[9]

In public Frida appeared proud and confident of herself. She had a powerful presence. Her dress and her demeanor, however, disguised a despair, an uncertainty, and a woundedness that grew after her marriage to Diego Rivera. She didn't talk with others about her inner world or her pain, but she expressed it in her art.

Near the dress is a woman in the water with a rope being drawn tightly around her neck by a male figure with a mask. He represents Chac Mool, an ancient pre-Hispanic figure on whom sacrificial subjects, often women,[10] were prepared for a bloody ritual of ripping out the heart. He is a negative animus who has no feeling for her, reminiscent of the Robber Bridegroom in the Grimms' fairy tale by that name. Frida's relationships with men were mostly problematic, and she often felt that they, especially Diego, ripped her heart out. In the painting, the father and mother have their backs turned and don't see the imminent threat and danger to Frida, and indeed, Frida felt neglected and abandoned all her life.

---

9 Helga Prignitz-Poda, *Frida Kahlo: The Painter and Her Work* (Munich: Schirmer/Mosel Publishers, 2004), 31.

10 Mark Cartwright, "Aztec Sacrifice," *Ancient History Encyclopedia*, September 2, 2013, http://www.ancient.eu/Aztec_Sacrifice/.

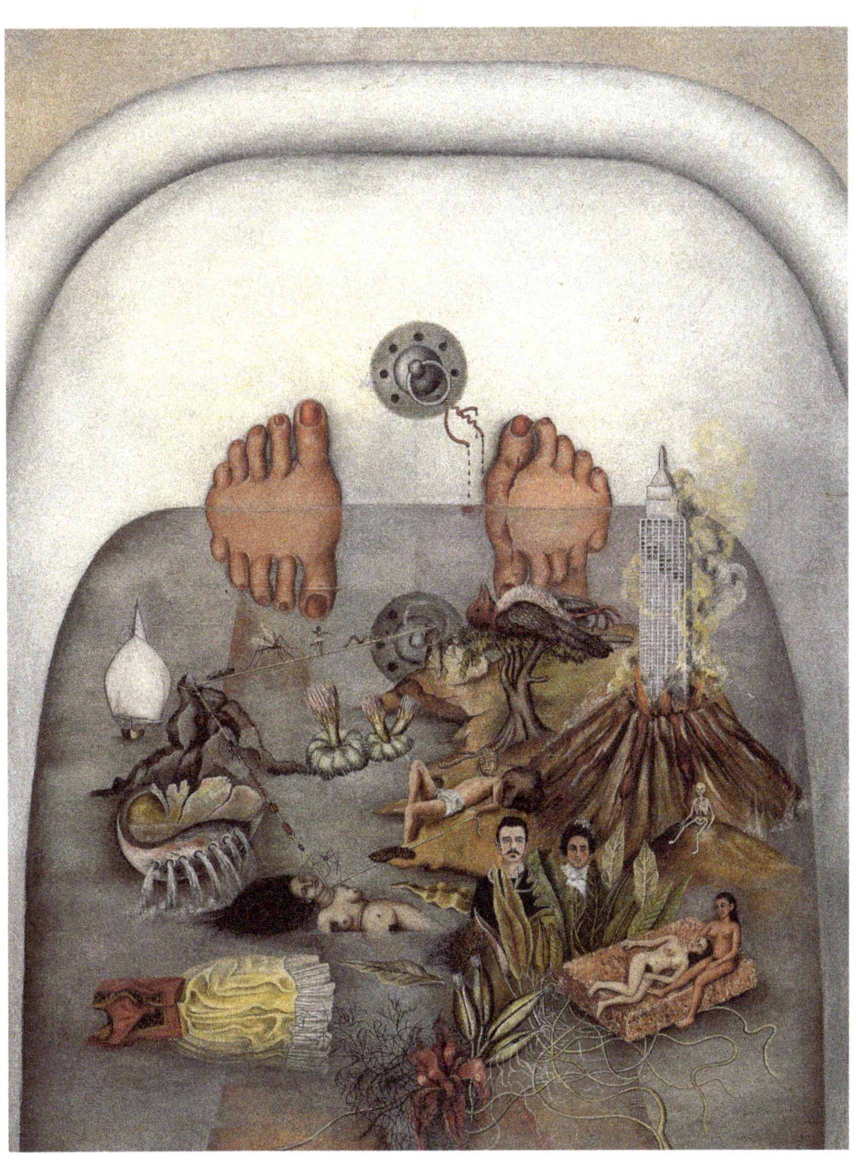

Figure 1: "What I Saw in the Water" by Frida Kahlo © 2016 Banco de México Diego Rivera Frida Kahlo Museums Trust, Mexico, D.F. / Artists Rights Society (ARS), New York.

The next painting (Figure 2) is called *The Two Fridas*. This was painted soon after Frida's divorce from Diego. From Frida's diaries we know that she had an imaginary girlfriend from an early age. When things were difficult, she would escape to the other Frida. One of her favorite poems was one by Goethe called "Ginkgo Biloba." It ends with the lines:

> In my songs do you not feel
> That at once I'm one and double?[11]

One Frida seemed to be shaped by early childhood, where women were in the traditional role of wife and mother, dependent upon husbands for support; the other by a Frida who was confident, free, and independent, in a less conventional role where she pursued her individual interests. She wrestled with these two Fridas increasingly as she got older.

---

11 Johann Wolfgang von Goethe, "Gingko Biloba," in *Selected Poems, Volume 1*, ed. Christopher Middleton (Princeton, NJ: Princeton University Press, 1983), 209.

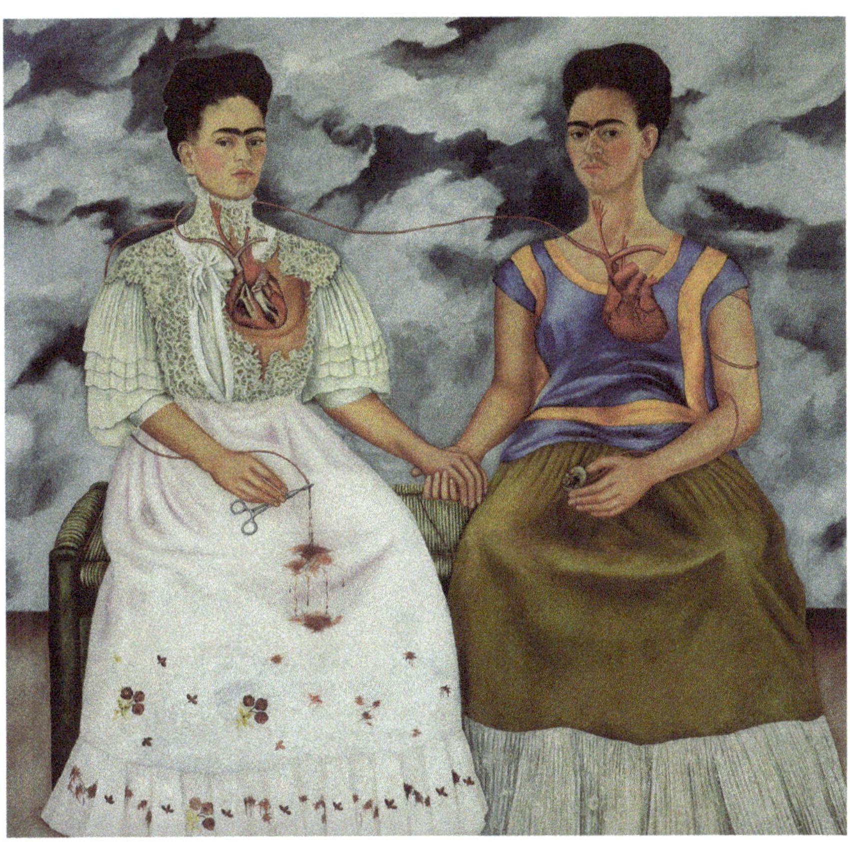

Figure 2: "The Two Fridas" 1939 by Frida Kahlo © 2016 Banco de México Diego Rivera Frida Kahlo Museums Trust, Mexico, D.F. / Artists Rights Society (ARS), New York.

The next painting (Figure 3) is called *Me and My Parrots*. Here we see Frida alone. The four parrots are Amazon parrots. We Jungians think of four as a symbol of wholeness. As we all know from Greek mythology, the Amazons were a clan of warlike women who lived in a matriarchal society and defended themselves against the male tribes surrounding them. They were not dependent upon men and were free to live their lives as they wished. The Tehuana dress Frida is wearing is the dress of women in Tehuantepec whose social organization is more like the Amazons. This painting was done after Frida's remarriage to Diego. But by then she had established herself as a talented artist in her own right, with commissions to support her independently. The union of male and female, which would render one more independent, fascinated Frida. This integration is symbolized by the ring portraying the lingam within the yoni.

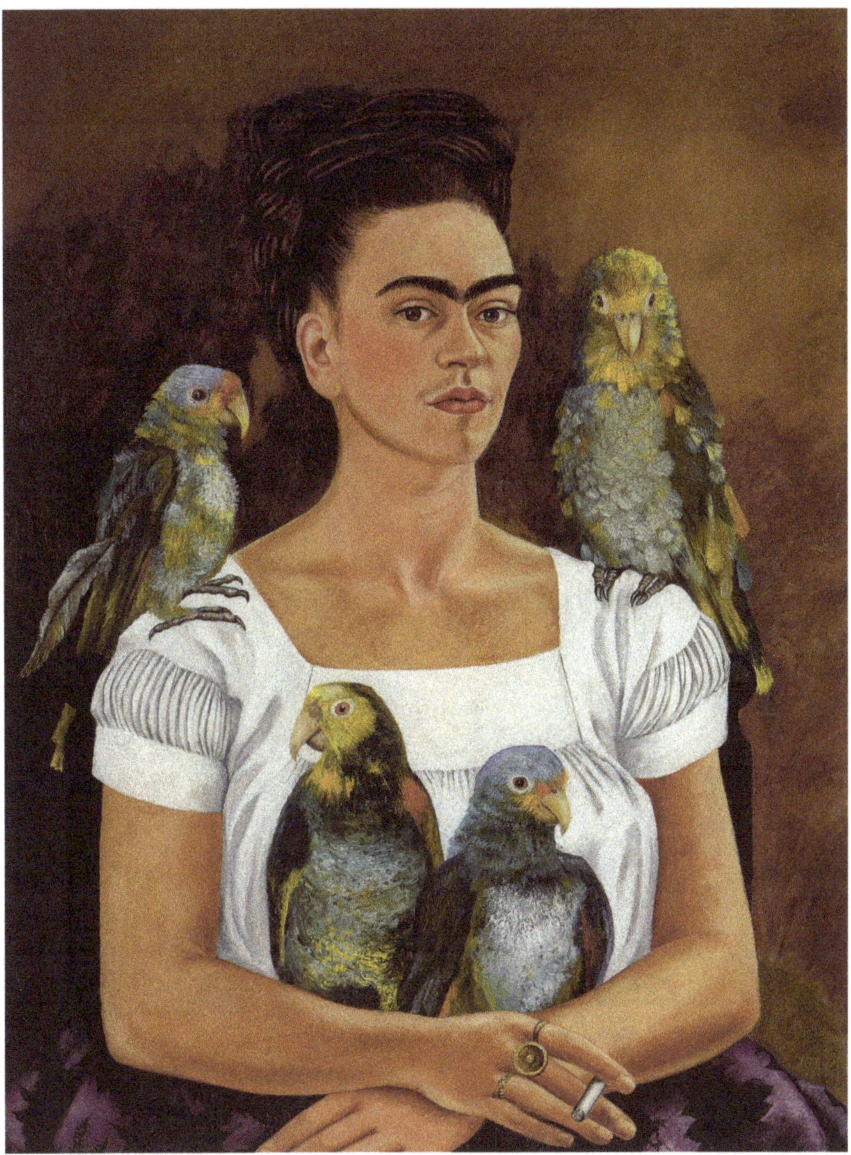

Figure 3: "Me And My Parrots" by Frida Kahlo © 2016 Banco de México Diego Rivera Frida Kahlo Museums Trust, Mexico, D.F. / Artists Rights Society (ARS), New York.

The next painting (Figure 4) is called *Self Portrait as a Tehuana or Diego in My Thoughts*. This painting suggests an integration of qualities she had previously seen as belonging to an outer Diego and incorporating them into her own psyche. Diego broke her heart repeatedly. He was independent and belonged only to himself, or so she believed. Transforming Diego into an inner figure of her psyche was a necessary step if Frida was to be free from the outer Diego and to belong to herself.

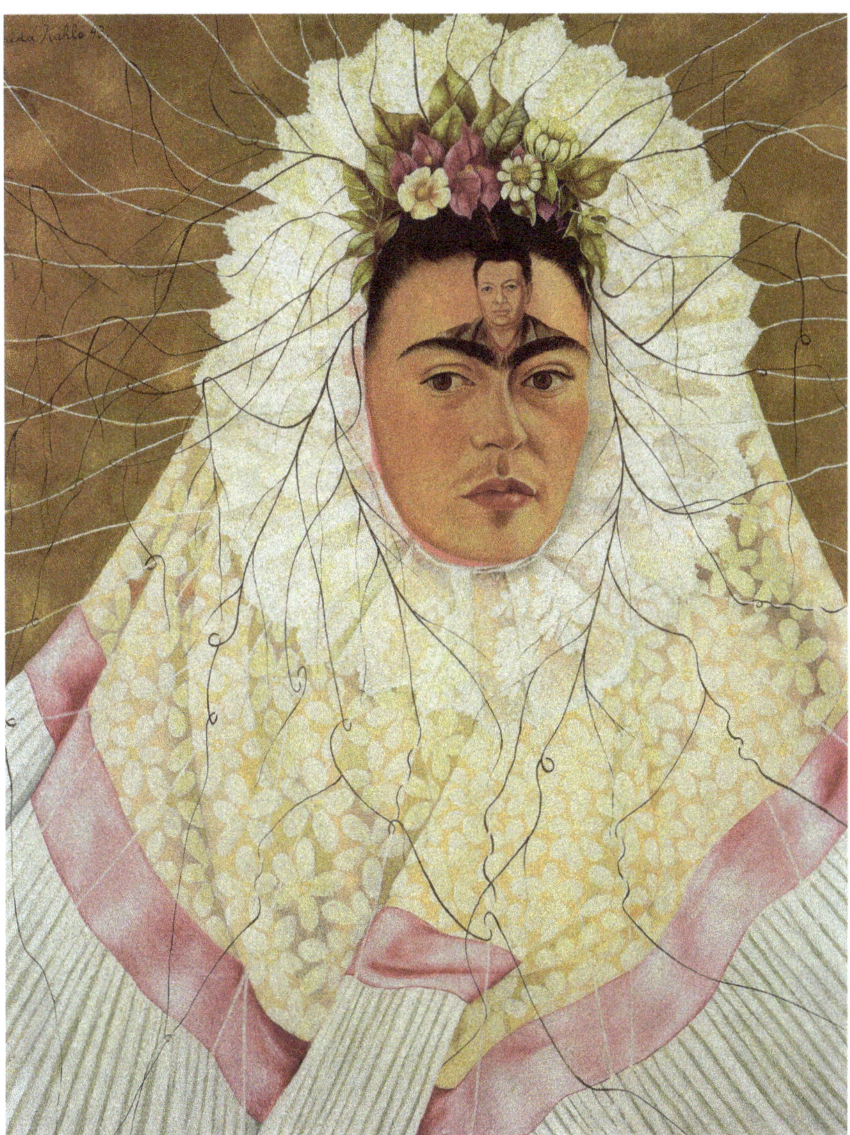

Figure 4: "Self Portrait As A Tehuna or Diego In My Thoughts" by Frida Kahlo, © 2016 Banco de México Diego Rivera Frida Kahlo Museums Trust, Mexico, D.F. / Artists Rights Society (ARS), New York.

The next painting (Figure 5) is called *The Broken Column*. Physically, the images correspond to Frida's medical reality, the bones and her spinal column which were broken in the tram accident when she was sixteen. She underwent repeated surgeries in which bones were broken and rebroken and doctors experimented with corsets and casts of different types in order to hold her together. The nails are wounds inflicted by Diego. Prignitz-Poda notes that: "To be nailed, *estar clavado*, in colloquial Mexican Spanish means 'to be cheated on.'"[12] The tears she shows in her painting were never shown in reality in public. In actual life, she disguised both her physical and psychological suffering. The painting clearly symbolized through the images of her body some desperate attempt to hold together a broken inner and outer life, a problematic undertaking considering the large wounds life had inflicted on her.

––––––––––––––––––

12 Helga Prignitz-Poda, *Frida Kahlo: The Painter and Her Work* (Munich: Schirmer/Mosel Publishers, 2004), 210.

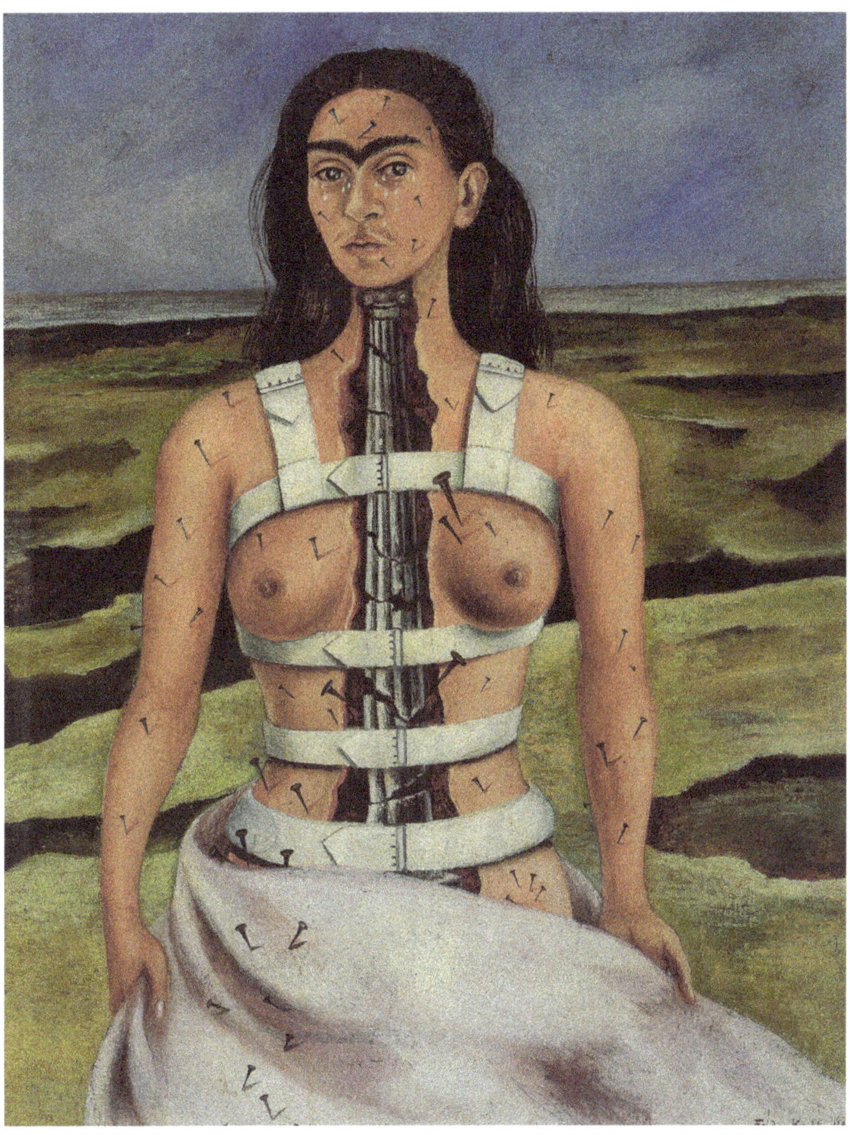

Figure 5: "The Broken Column" 1944 by Frida Kahlo © 2016 Banco de México Diego Rivera Frida Kahlo Museums Trust, Mexico, D.F. / Artists Rights Society (ARS), New York.

The last painting we will analyze is called *The Wounded Deer* (Figure 6). This painting appears to be one of the more dramatic portrayals of movement toward a yearned-for wholeness. It unites the animal world, reflected by the male deer, and the human world, represented by Frida's head. It also integrates the masculine and the feminine. Mythologically, *The Wounded Deer* is associated with the story of Dido's inexpressible love for Aeneas and her betrayal by him, which was precipitated by Aeneas's sense of his destiny and his perceived duty to the gods. Driven insane by grief, Dido flees like a deer struck by an arrow. She commits suicide and wanders as a wounded deer through the forests of the under-world, unredeemed. Prignitz-Poda observes that "Frida adds to her signature the word 'Carma.' Every soul after death has to atone for the sins of life. It is hard to imagine a more powerful image for the longing to overcome the polar opposites,"[13] opposites such as male and female, human and instinctive, good and evil, and life and death. Prignitz-Poda suggests that Frida's longing likely included the longing for an end to all suffering and, we believe, her own redemption.

---

13 Helga Prignitz-Poda, *Frida Kahlo: The Painter and Her Work* (Munich: Schirmer/Mosel Publishers, 2004), 234.

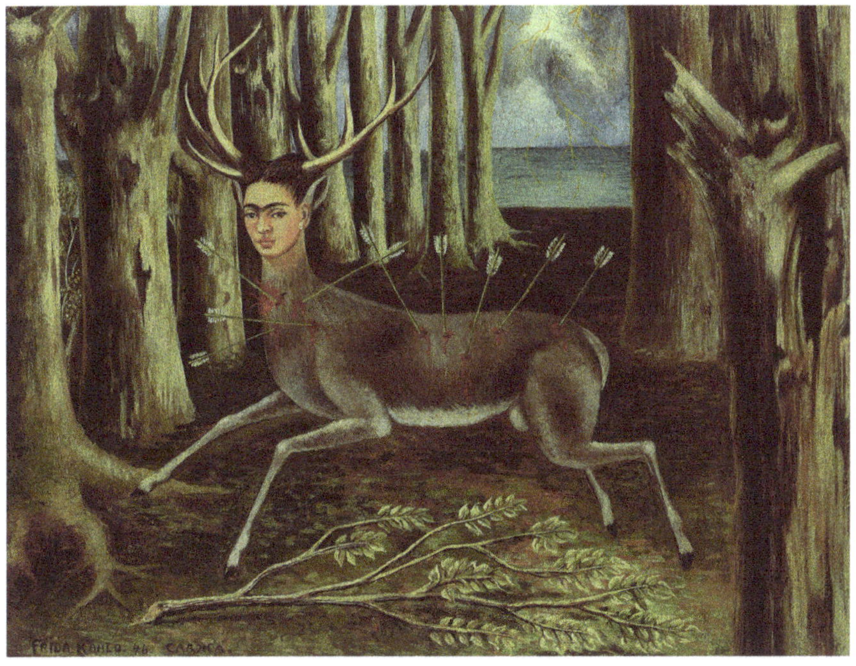

Figure 6: "The Wounded Deer or I Am A Poor Little Deer" 1946 by Frida Kahlo © 2016 Banco de México Diego Rivera Frida Kahlo Museums Trust, Mexico, D.F. / Artists Rights Society (ARS), New York.

Near the end of Frida's life, an exhibition composed solely of her works was being shown in Mexico. At the opening of the exhibit, Diego, her husband, gathered the crowd around him and spoke about his first meeting with Frida years earlier, while he was high on a scaffold, working on his murals:

> There was this skinny kid with these eyebrows shouting up at me, "Diego, I want to show you my paintings." But, of course, she made me come down to her, and I did, and I've never stopped looking. But I want to speak about Frida not as her husband, but as an artist. I admire her. Her work is acid and tender; hard as steel and fine as a butterfly's wing; lovable as a smile, cruel as the bitterness of life. I don't believe that ever before has a woman put such agonized poetry on canvas.[14]

One of the great benefits of creative work is that we don't have to go elsewhere to find meaning, wholeness, and fulfillment. We don't have to go outside to find a church or sacred place in order to discover and redeem ourselves. It starts between our ears and in our hearts and is projected onto our canvas or paper or other creative medium. Our art becomes a mirror of ourselves, just as the children we create are a partially reflected image of ourselves. Except in our art, both the mother and the father are inside of us, and we produce something that completely reflects ourselves. We begin to see ourselves in our work just as we see all artists in their work. It is only in this creative space, between our ears, in our imagination, that we are truly free. Otherwise, we are chained to the somber reality of the givens that obstinately shape and direct our lives.

Each visit to our keyboards or canvases is driven by our quest for wholeness and our obstinate wish to find ourselves and to be ourselves by expressing ourselves as completely as we can. And each creative step we gropingly take potentially draws us closer to ourselves, as it did for Frida.

---

14 *Frida*, directed by Julie Taymor (2002; Santa Monica, CA: Miramax Lionsgate, 2003), DVD.

II

DIVINE DISCONTENT:
THE INNER URGE TO CREATE

With Peter V. Emerson

Unhappiness and Creativity

We are born to create. We need to create. Fortunately, soon after we are born we encounter an unusual partner who helps us satisfy the need we have to leave our creative fingerprints on the world we briefly inhabit. This partner is called "Divine Discontent." It gets its name from a Faustian idea reflecting Goethe's view that unhappiness is the source of human creative energy, producing a constant striving that leads to the creation of culture and the world we live in.

We need unhappiness. It is an essential catalyst for creation and change. It makes us uncomfortable with things as they are. Our discomfort, then, prods us into the creative activity necessary to transform things as they are into things we hope will be better. Imagine a world in which we had miraculously become happy all the time. Why would we want to risk changing a single thing? Fortunately, nature provides an abundance of the discontent that we need but don't want. Of course, there are many qualities that contribute to progress and change. Certainly, curiosity and intelligence are prominent among them. Without some energizing drive, however, curiosity becomes idle, intelligence languishes, and change becomes modest at best.

Generally we are unaware of the paradox that it is unhappiness that actually drives our urge toward happiness. We have to go through unhappiness to get to happiness. Unhappiness runs the show. It is so unpleasant and uncomfortable that we spend significant portions of our lives and our energy creating and achieving things we have been taught will make us happy and, thereby, permit us to break free of the pain of our discontent. From very early in life, parents, society, books, and even advertising have influenced our beliefs about what would make us happy: good grades, good friends, lettering in a sport, getting into the college of our choice, falling in love, getting married, having children, finding the right job, getting promoted, making a lot of money, writing a novel, becoming famous, and on and on. It is quite true that all these things can make us happy for a while. The belief, however, that we can somehow live in a continuous state of happiness is an illusion. When unhappiness inevitably returns, we identify once more something we believe will make us happy and once again attempt to achieve it. The collective result of all these achievements creates, as Goethe believed, the portion that humans contribute to the continuously changing world we live in.

This is not intended exclusively as a paean to unhappiness. Rather, it attempts to right the balance by offering the view that, in the pantheon of feelings, unhappiness is at least as important as happiness. Nor do we intend to diminish the importance of happiness. No one yearns for unhappiness. Everyone yearns for happiness. Understandably, happiness gets the better press. We prefer happiness because we prefer pleasure to pain. We tend to interpret feeling happy as proof that we are living life successfully. We're making right choices. The truth is, if we never tasted happiness, the unhappiness that causes us to work and sweat to create the things that we believe will make us happy would be a cruel hoax. Still, despite all the objective reasons for an equivalent importance for happiness and unhappiness, if it were left up to us, we would almost certainly forgo Goethe's spinach and choose to be happy all the time.

The Declaration of Independence of the United States reflects the powerful valuation accorded the ideal of happiness. Its valuation is so high that happiness is ranked along with life and liberty as the three rights with which our Creator has endowed us. Interestingly, Jefferson phrased this right as the "pursuit of happiness," not its attainment. One could wonder if Jefferson believed that achieving and actually maintaining happiness would be detrimental to the creative effort that must unfold, if America were to grow as he hoped. It's the absence of happiness that makes us pursue it. We don't need to pursue something we already have.

This positive valuation of happiness leads to an equally negative valuation of unhappiness, so much so that a cultural bias approaching the force of a taboo is applied to unhappiness. The pressure to be happy is so strong that it is difficult to even acknowledge when one in fact feels unhappy. The compulsion to be happy, or, at least to appear happy, is insidious. Even married couples are reluctant to broach the subject of their unhappiness. The spouse we reveal it to can feel threatened and worry that his/her partner's unhappiness is because of something he or she has done or failed to do. This taboo is expressed beautifully in the television series, *Mad Men*.[15] The doctor of Draper's beautiful wife has told her that he can find nothing physically wrong with her. He suggests she might consider seeing a psychiatrist. In bed with her husband, she repeats what her doctor said and asks her husband if he thinks she should see a psychiatrist. He replies that the only people he knew who went to psychiatrists were unhappy. Then, he asks her if she is unhappy. "Of course I'm happy," she replies.

Much unhappiness lies below the threshold of consciousness. We feel guilty if we feel unhappy because we interpret the feeling as meaning we have somehow failed. We are afraid of this feeling and repress it. Imagine that one of us has six children to feed and educate and a huge mortgage. We may be very unhappy in our job but repress that feeling because to acknowledge it consciously and name it would threaten our existence. Unconscious as the feeling may be, it, nevertheless, drives us to identify and create some mode of existence we believe would make us happy.

Despite deeply ingrained ideals that drive our strong preference for happiness, the reality is that nature has wired us psychologically in a way that assures we experience sufficient "Divine Discontent" to sustain and promote creation. For one thing, it has made happiness ephemeral, like

---

15 *Mad Men*, "Ladies Room," TV Series, directed by Matthew Weiner (2007; Santa Monica, CA: Lionsgate, 2008.), DVD.

other feelings. Happiness is only one of a great number of feelings that compete for our conscious attention and our psychic space. Emotions of every stripe are constantly jostling and replacing each other. Anxiety, disappointment, anger, pain, pride, guilt, faith, doubt, hate, love, and many variations of these feelings come and go in a steady stream. Nature limits our power to choose or control feelings, especially strong ones. At some level, we can sense that they are quite autonomous. That doesn't keep us from trying to change them or minimize their pain and discomfort. Normally, however, we would find it impossible to feel happy when our child has died or our spouse has left us or we've just been fired. Or let us try to feel unhappy when we've just won the Olympic gold!

Some of our discontent also comes from the cards we are dealt at birth. For most of us, there is always something missing and always someone who appears to have drawn better cards with respect to health, wealth, status, connections, looks, size, physical and/or mental ability, geographic location, race, color, etc. We may be urged not to envy others and even wish not to, but we do. We are seldom entirely contented with our lot. Part of our discontent arises also from feeling inferior for what is missing and blaming ourselves for the situation, despite the obvious hand of fate. Envy and discontent are related. They both have to do with being unhappy with things as they are and with things we wish for but don't have.

This gap between the real and the ideal also reflects a sense that life is fundamentally asymptotic. An asymptote is a line that continuously approaches a given curve but does not meet it at any finite distance. That's what life is like. We spend our lives striving to get "there," but there is no permanent "there." There is just "almost there." We may briefly get close enough to "there" to experience what "there" might be like, as in orgasm, but we can't sustain it. When we think we have arrived at "there," we often imagine a still better or different "there" to strive for. Experiencing "there," even for a fleetingly brief moment, is key to the striving. It triggers our imagination and creativity to attempt to "get there and stay there." B. F. Skinner's rats may have had this experience when he fed them only randomly and intermittently. It kept them tapping the food lever. Tantalus is a mythological example of this phenomenon. From his name comes the word "tantalize." The Tantalus experience can be described as greatly desiring something that is just out of reach. And then there is the Moses experience. He got to see the Promised Land, but didn't get to go there. These are different faces of the asymptotic life. Not being able to get entirely "there" is a significant source of our unhappiness and discontent. Life energized by this productive process can seem cruel, but the results are arguably astounding. So are the costs. So are the fleeting moments of satisfaction, happiness, and even ecstasy. Feeling happy is one of the most beautiful and prized experiences in life. But it is beautiful and prized for the same reason that diamonds are. They are rare.

This asymptotic aspect of life and nature is apparent and expressed quite elegantly in our mathematics. The extremity of infinity cannot be reached mathematically by calculation. We can through calculation get ever closer to and approximate this value, but in the end we have to assume its existence. Despite this human limitation, we still make great progress by being able to come close, even if we don't actually get "there." Our calculations are good enough to get us to the moon. We just can't get to the end of the universe, which scientists believe continues to expand at a rapid rate. "There" is a moving target. If "there" existed and we could reach it permanently and hold on to it, creation would cease. There would be no need for creation, because we would be satisfied with what is. The desire to get "there" and the inability to do so are actually the source of the Divine Discontent that sustains creation.

Progress comes from the striving for an elusive happiness. And its elusiveness is precisely why it is prized. It is why we pursue it with great energy and focus. We strive arduously to achieve those things we believe will make us content. The striving does lead to achievement and moments of happiness, yes, but also to psychological problems. It can lead us to frenetic, obsessive-compulsive behaviors that burden us with stress and, not infrequently, addiction. In the process of pursuing happiness, we often stumble onto drugs, alcohol, gambling, and other addictions that more quickly and easily make us happy, until they inevitably don't. Then, we turn to religion or therapy to help us escape our unhappiness.

Therapy doesn't turn out so well, either, when it comes to making us happy. We, of course, hope that therapy will help us find this elusive happiness. Unfortunately, we will be disappointed unless we are able eventually to see happiness in a different light. Therapy is unable to do for us what all our achievements have also been unable to do. It will not be able to annihilate unhappiness; nor should it. An important part of the "cure," if we need a "cure," is to comprehend that happiness is an experience that comes and goes in everyone's life. It is perfectly human and normal to experience feelings other than happiness a significant part of the time. In our society there is a strong and ubiquitous pressure to be happy, and it can be a great relief simply to realize that nature didn't intend us to continuously be so. Unhappiness does not mean we've failed; it simply means we're human. We also need to grasp the irony that happiness itself, if it were a prolonged experience, would actually be a threat to our growth, development, and creativity. We need to accept that the creation of our culture, like the creation of a child, cannot be accomplished without considerable pain, labor, and difficulty. Unhappiness is one of the largest components of the price we pay to purchase the world in which we live. This essential cost creates a huge dilemma, because we want the beneficial results of unhappiness without its pain. We forget the refrain of the old song whose title is, "If You Want the Rainbow, You Must Have the Rain." As one patient was ending a long therapy, he simply concluded, "Well, I guess you just have to learn to grin and bear it."

Finally, while therapy clearly does not help us find happiness, it may, if we work hard at it and have a bit of luck, help us find something more important. It may help us find meaning in our lives, help us find what is truly important to us. This could be a welcome outcome. As Dr. Carl Jung once pointed out, we can endure any of life's difficulties, unhappiness, and suffering as long as it has meaning.[16]

---

16 This comment was attributed to C.G. Jung by the late C. Toni Frey-Wehrlin, a Jungian analyst in Zürich who helped establish the Zürichberg Clinic.

The Pursuit of Meaning

While it may not be entirely true, it feels as if aging, with all its difficulties, brings with it a mounting share of unhappiness. For this reason, as we age, the pursuit of meaning becomes increasingly important to our health and well-being. With age comes the steady diminution of the faculties we need in order to experience even fleeting contentment and pleasure. Life becomes more limited as our vision, our hearing, our taste, and our sexuality diminish. More and more things begin to hurt. If we can't believe we are doing something meaningful and important in life, we could easily conclude all the suffering from declining health and strength is not worth it. This has its obvious dangers. Without meaning, we might not be able to endure.

However, even if we accept that we need to do something meaningful in our lives, we still face the challenge of finding what on earth that might be. When we were in harness in our work, whether work was at home raising children or at the office following one's profession, or both, we probably felt some degree of meaning from what we did. But when we retire, we don't have our work to give us that meaning. Do we have to write a book? Compose a symphony? Win the senior golf or tennis tournament? Volunteer for meals on wheels? Give blood? Help a disabled son, daughter, or grandchild? Serve on the vestry? Get into politics? Support and even demonstrate for good causes? Reading trashy novels, watching trashy TV, or even seeing beautiful sunsets probably won't do it for us, even if in the abstract we think we may have earned the right to do so.

Making our task more difficult and problematic is the fact that even when we conclude we need to do something significant with our lives, we have to figure it out for ourselves. What seems to be of great value for one person may not be for another. We may feel we would be doing something worthwhile if we wrote a best-selling book. Then, we remember someone like Hemingway, who won the Nobel Prize for Literature and then killed himself. Or we may think of people like Darwin or Carnegie, both of whom spent the latter part of their lives struggling with guilt over the very achievements that made them famous. Clearly, we aren't necessarily safe even if we are doing something with our lives that is considered worthwhile by the collective society. This latter point is sadly illustrated in the poem, "Richard Cory."[17] It's the story of a man who had all the admirable qualities of which his collective society approved, yet, he shot himself in the prime of life. The meaning of a human life is a pretty subjective valuation, and apparently we are on our own when it comes to finding it. If, like Hemingway or Richard Cory, we don't believe that our life and what we are doing with it is important, then it isn't.

It is psychologically important to believe in what we are doing. If others consider something to be meaningful but it doesn't feel meaningful to us, it doesn't matter. And if we as individuals feel something is of value, it doesn't really matter what others feel. Photographing sunsets, painting palm trees, weaving baskets, supporting causes, laughing with friends, writing memoirs, or many other less-than-earth-shaking activities may seem pretty wasteful or worthless to others. But they may sustain the individuals who do them as long as they feel they are meaningful. Still, it may well take something also deemed significant by the collective society to satisfy our need for meaning.

Meaning and the Pursuit of Interests

Since we need meaning to bear the unavoidable unhappiness and suffering we are bound to experience, especially in old age, how do we find it? We can't just decide we want to find something valuable to us and have it magically appear. Here's one way: if we want to find out what is meaningful and important to a child, we watch what interests him or her. We watch where his or her attention goes, what he is drawn to. Steven Spielberg's parents did this with him. They watched very keenly what interested him and what he liked. It turned out he really liked cameras. And for him, what he liked and what most interested him turned out also to be very meaningful in his life.

If we want to find what we might value, then, we must do for ourselves what we would do for a child, what Spielberg's parents did for

---

17 Edwin Arlington Robinson, "Richard Cory," *The Poetry Foundation*, 1897, http://www.poetryfoundation.org/poems-and-poets/poems/detail/44982.

him. We have to watch ourselves like a hawk. Journaling can be an enormously helpful tool in this regard. We cannot journal without paying attention to ourselves.

If we attend to and notice what interests us, what we like and dislike, we will be led to what is meaningful and important to us, just as Spielberg was. (Of course, Spielberg, like all of us, had problems growing up, but mirroring of meaningful interests was not one of them.) Like artists, we pay attention to the subject we wish to paint or write about. In our case, we are the subjects. As we portray each new detail of our selves, a picture gradually emerges that shows us who we are. It takes patience. Just as the meaning of a painting cannot be discerned with the first brushstrokes, so too the fullness of our meaning appears only as the details of our inner selves slowly emerge, until they reach a clarifying, critical mass.

The suggestion to pay careful attention to our selves isn't about narcissistic self-absorption. It's about a relationship to our selves, a relationship between two parts of our selves in which one part is the observer and the other the observed. What we mean by paying attention is a brief, daily process in which we attempt to become more conscious of our selves by observing thoughts and feelings that normally stream through our minds unnoticed but that contain important information that helps add to our knowledge of who we are, what interests us, and what doesn't.

The process is enhanced if we carry a small notebook or 3x5 cards (or whatever we choose) with us wherever we go. When we have a particular thought or feeling that catches our attention, we write it down. (If we wait until the end of the day to note these thoughts and feelings, we can forget many of the important details.) Then, when we sit down for our journaling session, we have access to the information we captured at the moment of experience. It takes a long time to acquire all the pieces of our puzzle, but when we do so, we become the world's leading expert on our own thoughts and feelings. It's both a good and essential investment.

There are some other benefits from journaling. The necessary unhappiness in our lives can create a lot of stress, tension, and even guilt that puts pressure on our minds and emotions. Such pressure can make us sick if we don't find ways to relieve it. Journaling serves as a kind of psychic cathartic, a psychic bowel movement, if we may, that clears out psychic detritus that otherwise could become as toxic as backed-up bowels. Unhappiness, like food, is essential for our well-being, but we need to deal with the undigested and unassimilated contents if we are to stay healthy. A cathartic effect similar to journaling can also be achieved by a kind of confession in which we divulge inner contents to a trusted and nonjudgmental priest, therapist, or friend, instead of expelling them onto a receptive and nonjudgmental page. Journaling, of course, is a way to obtain the cathartic effect on our own.

Becoming conscious of our interests is not an easy task. For one thing, there are often multiple and competing interests that have to be differentiated and prioritized before they can be useful to us. Despite the difficulty, the process is essential to finding our inner guidance system. Throughout our lives it empowers, centers, and sustains us when we can form theories of meaning about what affects and shapes us.

Meaning won't cure the unhappiness we experience in life. Nothing will. Unhappiness is too essential to life. However, we do know how we feel when we are doing something that is important to us. We feel energy. The energy doesn't abolish our unhappiness, but it is a pretty good remedy for exhaustion and depression.

Meaning and a Connection to Something Bigger Than Ourselves

Humans are dependent beings. We are profoundly dependent upon both nature and others for our survival. We neither possess nor control much of what we need to support us on life's journey. Some deep part of us knows how dependent, powerless, and vulnerable we really are. But it is this unconscious truth about our weakness that draws us inexorably toward something bigger than our small selves.

To the extent that we sense these deep feelings, we have to keep them to ourselves if we are beyond childhood. It is unacceptable to give voice to them. We sound like we have no will or backbone. We haven't made the right choice, which is to be strong. To say, "I feel helpless," is to sound like a child. We repress these unacceptable feelings. But they don't go away. They just go underground, where they do their work in the dark. We experience them as free-floating anxiety, as restlessness and uneasiness to which we can assign no specific cause. We assert our strength, confidence, and independence while feeling, even if vaguely, quite the opposite. We wear a mask that conceals an important part of our truth.

These feelings of powerlessness are by no means limited to people who fail; paradoxically, the highly successful can also be assailed by them. This paradox is illustrated in the following stories of two men we worked with who, on the surface, seem almost opposite. Dan is a therapist who had worked his way up to head a large mental health hospital. He got fired and tried to go back to being a therapist. He was introverted and depressed. He had little energy for building a private therapy practice. His COBRA insurance was running out, and he soon would not have enough money to pay his mortgage. He really didn't feel like doing anything. He had few friends and connections. He seemed to have no particular interests except, perhaps, writing, but he certainly couldn't make a living from that. His wife did volunteer work. She was very critical of him and, understandably, afraid. Dan, of course, was very anxious. Time and money were running out, and he felt powerless to do anything about it.

Jack, on the other hand, was a political appointee. He was extraverted with enormous energy for work. He was well connected and a frequent guest on network talk shows. He was married to a very bright and successful woman. Jack worked extremely hard and for long hours. For recreation he drank, picked up women, and looked at porn. His wife had caught him looking at porn and having affairs. She was angry but stuck with him. He drank enough to have blackouts and was frightened by some of his own outrageous behavior. He was afraid that, if some of his drunken behavior became public, he would lose his position of power and his partner. And he was terrified by his inability to control his drinking and his sexual behavior. He simply could not understand why he could not stop putting himself at risk.

These two men seem on the surface to be quite different, even opposites of one another. As the world sees them, one is very successful, and the other appears to be a failure. But at some deeper level they have similarities. Both are frightened by their powerlessness to control their behavior. Neither can control his behavior in a way that would appear to serve his self-interest. Jack cannot stop behavior that is against his self-interest, while Dan cannot start behavior that would serve his self-interest. Deep down, they are both unhappy, feel much guilt about their behavior, feel powerless to change in a positive direction, and are very anxious and afraid. One seems to be afraid of losing what he has, and the other feels powerless to acquire what he needs. At the visceral, feeling level, their experience is identical, despite the huge differences in outer life. No matter how different we seem to those on the outside, we may be quite alike on the inside.

It's the powerlessness to control behavior that appears to lie behind the anxiety and guilt. One feels anxious and guilty about risking what he has; the other feels anxious and guilty about not being able to get what he wants. They both feel weak. They both feel threatened by an inability: in one case, the inability to act, and in the other case, the inability to stop acting. One is rendered powerless by what he must do; the other is rendered powerless by what he can't do. The experience of powerlessness seems to be the common denominator for two otherwise opposite persons. The feeling that I am powerless to do something I should do, or powerless to not do something I shouldn't do, is terrifying, guilt-inducing, and humbling.

The anxiety and guilt that such feelings of helplessness induce, not only in Dan and Jack but also in all of us, can actually transform us and empower us, if we can acknowledge them and arrive at the truth that all humans share these feelings and have difficulty becoming conscious of them and admitting them. We know that at the deepest level humans are alike chemically and biologically. Both Dan's and Jack's stories suggest that at this deep level, we may also be alike psychologically. If we look at Jack and Dan deeply enough to get beneath surface appearances, we find helplessness.

If they each had the insight, Dan and Jack could say that "I am that" about their chemical composition. In the same way, if they chose to look within, they could say "I am that" about their own helplessness. They could say of one another that "you are that," and, joining their voices, they could say in unison, "we are that." If all humans became conscious that "we are that," our feeling of helplessness could become powerfully uniting, bridging many of the differences between peoples. It could change our relationship to one another. How could we hurt one another, if we each knew that "we are that"? We would understand that we would be hurting our own selves. The greatly undervalued quality of helplessness, shared by all of us, might become like the stone rejected by the builders, becoming the headstone of an arch that holds us all together and serves to form a more perfect union. In helplessness, the opposites become united.

For this reason, the acknowledgment of powerlessness is an essential step in gaining power. Recovering alcoholics have to learn this. They have to admit their powerlessness over alcohol before they can find the strength to stop drinking. They can find their way to strength by admitting their own weakness. It's just as we saw with unhappiness: we have to go through one opposite to find our way to the other.

This same phenomenon is on view in a recent movie called *High Strung*.[18] In the film, a ballet student says to her teacher, "I just want to be perfect." The teacher asks, "And what happens when you achieve perfection? You stop then? It's imperfection that keeps us alive, motivating us to push further and further."

The powerlessness that we experience in life also seems to be connected somehow with how well-aligned and how much in accord the ego is with the Self.[19] When there is a conflict between "my will be done" and "thy will be done," "thy will be done" tends to win. As Jung puts it, "Just

---

18 *High Strung*, directed by Michael Damian (2016; Leeds, UK: Riviera Films, LLC, and High Strung, LLC, 2016), https://www.netflix.com/title/80098201.

19 The word "Self" is a Jungian construct meaning, we believe, something roughly equivalent to the word God, as it appears in any language. In fact, Jung stated that the Self "might equally well be called the 'God within.'" (C.G. Jung, 1967. "The Mana-Personality," CW 7, ¶ 399.) When we refer to God, we mean to include all the conceptions of God that suggest the deepest unity that originates and sustains creation, whether God is a he, she, or it or whether a light, a word, a thought, a person, pure reason, pure energy, a cell, a particle, a wave, a string, natural selection, infinity, among many other possibilities.

as circumstances or outside events happen to us and limit our freedom, so the self acts upon the ego like an objective occurrence which free will can do little to alter."[20] These two men seem to be experiencing this conflict. They appear to want something the Self is opposed to. They feel both thwarted and threatened by a power greater than themselves. They will behave compulsively until they give up their resistance to it and figure out what the Self wants them to do, rather than what the ego thinks they "ought" to do. They will only feel empowered when their energy flows along a gradient chosen by the Self.

Jung believed that, for a man, it is the anima that leads him to himself. It is his feminine side, expressed as relatedness, feeling, and interest, that guides him toward himself. This is not easy to do and requires enormous attention to one's own feelings and interests. Men are more likely to pay attention to their thoughts for guidance and to look down on feelings and interests that are in conflict with them. For example, Jack had a dream about shit in bathroom pipes spewing all over him. From his very one-sidedly masculine way, he probably sees feelings as shit, something worthless that you turn your nose up to. Dan appears to be equally contemptuous of his own feelings. They assume feelings will lead you into trouble rather than lead you out of it. They look down on the very thing that may save them. As Jung has written, "Hence, it is practically impossible to get a man who is afraid of his own femininity to understand what is meant by anima."[21]

We have wondered why the Self renders us helpless. The only thing we can think of is that God knows that we, unconsciously, of course, will feel we are God as long as we are successful at everything we do. This inflated feeling is a result of an unconscious identification with the Godhead. Until the ego is humbled, it won't turn to God. It resists acknowledging something larger than itself. It probably isn't truly capable of being open to the Self. The failure of will seems to be the thing that actually connects one to God. Only when the ego has failed can it bend its knee enough to genuinely connect with God.

---

20 C.G. Jung, 1969. "The Ego," CW 9ii, ¶ 9.
21 C.G. Jung, 1969. "On the Psychology of the Trickster-Figure," CW 9i, ¶ 485.

Becoming connected to something bigger than ourselves endows us with meaning that sustains us through life's pain and difficulties. This connection is meaningful to us because we draw strength, courage, and security from it. As a result, as we embrace this larger entity, we gain confidence in handling our problems so that many difficulties that once hijacked our attention and our energy recede in importance. For example, the American colonists almost certainly had a feeling of increased security when they joined together to form the United States. They joined into community for strength, security, support, and safety, knowing that their community was stronger, more secure, more supportive, and safer than the individuals that comprised it; the community became for them a power greater than themselves individually. Another example that is well known is when President Kennedy made his "*Ich bin ein Berliner*" speech. Berlin was divided into four parts and surrounded by hostile Soviet forces. Berliners felt relieved, even saved, by Kennedy's promise to support and protect them.

It is the feeling that came to the people of England in World War II when America entered the war. They had felt threatened with annihilation by the Germans, but America's entry almost overnight transformed that desperate feeling into one of security and hope. They felt connected to, supported by, and protected by something bigger than themselves. Churchill acknowledged the transformative effect of America's entry into the war. Benefitting from a connection to a power greater than ourselves, is, of course, an ancient religious belief.

An insistent drive for survival leads life to create processes that protect it against extinction. An important part of the defense against these threats is a tendency for the smallest elemental particles to connect with each other in order to form increasingly larger entities. Subatomic particles join to form atoms, then atoms join to form molecules, and then molecules combine to become the building blocks of all of physical life. Similarly, letters form words, words form sentences, sentences form paragraphs, and the paragraphs create a book, and, ultimately, world literature. Individual brushstrokes join to become a painting, and individual notes join to become music.

We detect this same tendency in the way humans organize. Earliest life consisted of individuals living in isolation. Then, to gain greater security, they coupled, and then formed families, which, in turn, formed tribes. The units eventually formed into city states, nations, and regions like the Euro Zone. Logic would lead us to think that the ultimate object of the increasingly larger units is world government. These bigger entities may become so meaningful and important that we become willing to sacrifice our autonomy and even ourselves in order to preserve them. Nature appears to be set up so that, although individuals may perish, the species is sacrosanct and must be preserved at all costs. It preserves itself with collective strength.

It also appears that nature attempts to preserve the species by implanting in the individual an instinct to sacrifice himself when the entity to which he belongs is sufficiently threatened. There are many examples of this phenomenon. During World War II, the Japanese kamikaze attacks increased exponentially as the threat to the homeland grew nearer. It's as if the instinct for individuals to sacrifice themselves for a greater good is proportionate to the threat to whatever their greater good is. This instinct appears to be akin to the maternal instinct of a mother bear when her cubs are threatened.

The need for meaning and its power in our lives can also be seen in modern examples like ISIS and the willingness of its adherents to sacrifice themselves. Most people find meaning from work or activity that saves lives or helps others. But the need for meaning is so deep that, if it isn't found in saving lives or helping others, it may be found in taking lives. If meaning is sufficiently powerful to cause us to sacrifice our lives, it is easily powerful enough to help us bear the inevitable unhappiness and difficulties of life.

At some time in our lives, many of us have worked a jigsaw puzzle. It's a pretty good metaphor for the psychological process of searching for and discovering meaning by connecting smaller pieces to something bigger. It has to do with our identity. It has to do with who we are. Does our meaning come from being a single piece? From being a single piece connected to some of the other pieces? Or does it come from being connected to the whole thing?

When we see all the disconnected pieces of the puzzle, before seeing a picture of what it is supposed to be, we can't identify what it is. We don't know what it means. We don't really know whether it is a farm house in Provence or the cathedral at Chartres. We don't know whether it is something ordinary or unique. We start with one piece and look for the neighboring ones in order to discover the identity and meaning of the whole thing.

At the very beginning of life, we are whole. All the pieces are there in potentia. As soon as ego consciousness is born and the process of socialization sets in, wholeness is lost. Large parts of ourselves that parents and conventional society disapprove of get repressed or are not allowed to appear or be expressed. We get narrowed down to what is permissible. The yearning for the lost parts of ourselves gets increasingly stronger until at midlife, the forbidden parts often roar out of the unconscious. It can cause our families and us a lot of problems. We know it as the midlife crisis. Our lives have come to feel meaningless and empty because much of us is inaccessible. We're like a partially completed puzzle that has no identity and for which we haven't yet discovered a meaning.

There is a specific aspect of socialization that particularly accounts for the growing loss of large parts of ourselves. It has to do with the way parents and society deal with what we call the problem of the opposites. Pairs of opposites—love/hate, hot/cold, happiness/unhappiness—that appear very early in the development of the human psyche are indispensable to the operation of human awareness. Conscious awareness, and, therefore, human life as we know it, depends on the existence of these polar opposites. As Carl Jung wrote, "There is no consciousness without discrimination of opposites."[22]

These opposites are the elemental particles of our psychological make-up. Parents and society tend to prefer one side or the other of the pairs of opposites, whether it be order over disorder, timeliness over tardiness, or cleanliness over dirtiness, and so on. During socialization, what happens with one of the pairs of opposites happens with all the others. Whether the preference is subtle or glaringly obvious, we become conditioned to

---

22 C.G. Jung, 1969. "Psychological Aspects of the Mother Archetype," CW
   9i, ¶ 178.

favor one of the members of each and all of the pairs of opposites. It's as if we reach adulthood with these preferences imprinted on our minds. In this fashion, all the opposites carry a negative or positive charge in our psyches in varying degrees. We lose touch with or even forget the importance of the most negatively charged opposites. These become our missing parts, which are difficult to access. Their minimization is a threat to meaning. No half of any pair of opposites means anything without its contrasting half. While, for example, neither happiness nor unhappiness has a meaning by itself, a powerful cultural taboo against unhappiness is a threat to the meaning of both. In order to achieve meaning, we have to recover these abandoned opposites, these missing pieces. It is crucial to the completion of our puzzle. Our one-sided preference for one or the other of the opposites brings clarity but leaves our puzzle incomplete. Clarity is gained at the expense of meaning. Meaning is more inclusive. It is more nuanced. It is "both/and" rather than "either/or." We yearn for that beginning state of wholeness we felt when we were connected to something bigger. And we spend the rest of our lives trying to find that bigger thing and reconnect with it.

If we are lucky and work hard at it, we begin to find our missing pieces and to restore and relate these desultory bits to the part that is already assembled. The work of discovering our bigger self can be facilitated and enhanced by steps we can take, like honoring our interests, journaling, and creative activity. A good therapist can also help by reflecting back to us parts of ourselves that are revealed in our talk and our dreams. Usually this work doesn't begin in earnest until midlife. As more and more pieces are added, we begin to realize who we are. We begin gropingly to experience our emerging identity. We begin to find what we mean just as we find what a puzzle means as more of its pieces are connected. Just as we gain security in the outer world by connecting with something bigger, so too in the inner world we gain strength and confidence by connecting to something bigger. The inner connection to something bigger may be even more important.

This is how we come to feel and experience that meaning in life depends upon this connection to something bigger than we are. We start with all the pieces. We pick up one of the pieces lying alone and apart from the others. It has no identity by itself. It means nothing alone. Then, we find where it belongs, where it relates to the bigger picture. At the moment we join the smaller piece to the larger thing, we experience a feeling of meaning. We realize the importance of both the part and the whole. No tiny piece can make the whole puzzle; no puzzle can be complete without the tiny piece. It's what we mean by fulfillment. What starts as perhaps an infinitesimal feeling of fullness at the beginning grows ever bigger as the process unfolds. In this process we may pick up pieces of other peoples' puzzles. These pieces have no meaning for us. They don't fit. They don't belong. Only when something belongs to and is related to our bigger self does it resonate with us and have meaning. Only then does it satisfy our hunger and fulfill us. If we attempt to fit pieces of other people's puzzles to our own, we experience an inner rejection mechanism that is, at least metaphorically, similar to what occurs at the physical level in organ transplants. There is a powerful resistance to what is not "us."

The urge to find and put together all our pieces is illustrated by a poem written by one of our patients who was struggling with his own identity crisis. We feel the poem is a poignant expression of the primal meaning of Divine Discontent: the return to self through an eternal yearning and striving that recollects the lost pieces of our self and redeems us by restoring us to our selves.

shattered bottles and ragtag pieces of broken hearts and people

> Sometimes I feel like a bottle
> That some angry drunk has hurled against a barroom wall
> And smashed to smithereens.
> And all those once related pieces scatter in a mess of shards
> Whose chaos mocks a former wholeness,
> Which vanished when it burst and fell.
> Some things are, perhaps, worth pasting back together,
> Some things, perhaps, are not.
> Is it worth it?
> That's hard to answer in the absolute.
> It depends on the pair of shoes you're standing in
> Or the pair of eyes you're looking through.

It depends, quite frankly, on whether you're the bottle or the shard,
Whether you're the angry drunk or some sensitive aesthete
Who looked with horror
As exquisite shape and form were suddenly reduced to artless rubble.
Through the bottle's eyes, yet another ox is gored.
It's no abstract question of shape or form.
It is something closer still.
It's a question of being a bottle or of being something else.
Shape or form or beauty mean nothing
When to be or not to be is the crucial question.
And shards, perhaps, would have a different stance.
For a shard, it's nothing special being connected to a nearby shard.
They're content to lie in desultory piles
In haughty isolation
That feels no need to touch or clasp adjacent things
To gain some sense of who they are.
A shard's a shard. And that is that.
And now,
Through Love's warm eyes appears another view
That has no special ax to grind with drunks or bottles or shards.
Love is love,
An ever-centripetal tendency that will not rest
Till shattered bottles and ragtag pieces of broken hearts and people
Are drawn once again and gathered in the place
Where first they started
And, at last, must dwell again.
Love is a completer of circles.
And with its caring hands picks from the barren floor
Each sharp but scraggly splinter,
And searches insistently for the neighboring pieces,
Which it patiently fits and joins till the puzzle is once again complete,
Even if it take to eternity.[23]

---

23 Used by permission.

Creative Work and the Connection to Something Bigger

There are a number of methods that can help us discover and connect the smaller pieces of our puzzles to the bigger entity. They would include work with dreams and various kinds of psychotherapy as well as religious practices like prayer and meditation. Among the variety of ways available to help us, we have found creative work, like the poem recited above, to be one of the most effective. We simply cannot do creative work without connecting to something bigger. Each successive brushstroke creates something larger that we are clearly connected to. Similarly, we add a sentence or paragraph to a book or article we are writing. We enlarge our business or even our house or garden and we have created something bigger. When we do that we not only connect with the creator within; we also come in contact with the container of all the creative processes that develop and sustain both our inner and outer worlds. All our creations carry our identity and mean something to us. They reflect who we are as much as a Rembrandt reflects who he was.

The creative processes that manifest as artistic structures, nature, and life in the outer world manifest as psychological structures, nature, and life in the inner world. Connecting with something bigger inside also increases confidence, strength, and feelings of security just as connecting with something bigger outside does. This increase in confidence and strength can empower us and give us the courage to express all of ourselves rather than the smaller part of ourselves that is approved by parents and society. Even in creative work, expressing all of ourselves can still be difficult and scary. It can cause us to be unhappy, as many artists know. But the connection to the bigger process gives us meaning, which helps us bear the hardships and unhappiness.

The medium we choose for creative work doesn't matter as long as it interests us. It's the creative process, not the particular medium, that helps us complete our puzzle and become who we are supposed to be. The simple process of doing creative work helps us discover unknown parts of ourselves and add them to our puzzle.

The reason why creative work helps us discover our missing pieces and connect them is that creative work requires the expression of all members of the pairs of opposites. For reasons associated with socialization as explained earlier, one member of all the pairs of opposites is more or less missing or inaccessible to us. Creative production in art, as in life, depends upon bringing two opposites, the masculine and the feminine, into close enough proximity to produce a "child" (i.e., a book, a symphony, a painting, etc.) without identifying solely with either of the opposites that created the "child." While the masculine and feminine opposites are fundamental to all creation, all the other opposites are important, too. It's hard to imagine writing or painting something if we were restricted to our conditioned preference for either the negative or the positive side of the opposites. What if we had to write using only light or dark, cold or warm, love or hate, war or peace? It would be bland and meaningless.

Drama, depth, and realness in all art is created by the appearance of opposites in close proximity—life/death, failure/success, loud/soft, fast/slow, point/counterpoint, light/dark, and straight/curved, for example. Straight-line sameness never produces drama unless it is compensated by crookedness or variety. The thrill and drama of the roller coaster is based on the same principle. We are pleasantly and steadily pulled to the highest point of the track, from which there is an unpleasant, scary, sudden drop toward the lowest point. It is in the transition between the heights and depths where the contrast and the thrill occur. The thrill comes from the contrast between the pleasure of going up and the fear of going down. The thrill, the rush, actually comes from the two opposites occurring in proximity to each other.

It is the drama created by the contrast and contradiction made possible by opposites that also draws us inexorably to movies (e.g., *Crash*,[24] *Lawrence of Arabia*,[25] or *A Civil Action*[26]) or to great art, literature, or

---

24 *Crash*, directed by Paul Haggis (2004; Santa Monica, CA: Lionsgate Films, 2005), DVD.

25 *Lawrence of Arabia*, directed by David Lean (1962; UK: Horizon Pictures, 2001), DVD.

26 *A Civil Action*, directed by Steven Zaillian (1998; Burbank, CA: Touchstone Pictures, 1999), DVD.

music (e.g., the opera *Tosca*[27] or the play *Hamlet*[28]). In *Tosca*, we see Scarpia, on his knees, praying in church, while leering lustfully at Tosca. In the movie, *Crash*, a policeman saves the life of a black woman he had humiliated and mistreated just days before. We see Hamlet being indecisive and cowardly one day, brave and sure the next. In *Lawrence of Arabia*, Lawrence risks his life to save a man he deliberately kills shortly thereafter. In *A Civil Action*, a greedy, money-driven, ambulance-chasing lawyer finds a cause for which he is willing to sacrifice his career and fortune. In *American Pastoral*,[29] Philip Roth portrayed a conventional family, so typical that it seemed archetypal, who nonetheless produced a daughter who joined the Weathermen underground group during the Vietnam War era. She led a life of rebellion, violence, and crime that contrasted sharply with all her family valued, leading eventually to the destruction of this formerly much-admired and successful family. To write this story, Roth had to access within himself these contrasting opposites, acknowledge them, and express them. That is, to write his story, he had to put himself in the shoes of and see through the eyes of his own rigid, conservative conventionality and his contrasting rebelliousness. By giving expression to the opposites in his writing, he could achieve the drama that results from these opposites in proximity. Another example is Peter, loving Christ one moment and denying him the next. There is a Jekyll and Hyde in all of us. We are drawn, as if against our will, to these conflicting, opposite portraits. We are drawn to them and have feeling for them because we see ourselves in them, whether we know it or not. We are drawn to images that reflect ourselves but also protect us from living through direct experience, with all its consequences. To know that we have the same base feelings in us as Scarpia, right alongside all of our goodness, is difficult to bear. Nevertheless, we are drawn to these characters and images because nature seems to have planted deep within us a developmental process that, through the agency of interest and feeling, attracts us irresistibly, drawing us closer

---

27 Giacomo Puccini, *Tosca* (Milan, Italy: Giulio Ricordi & Co., 1895).

28 William Shakespeare, *The Tragedy of Hamlet, Prince of Denmark*, accessed June 8, 2016, http://shakespeare.mit.edu/hamlet/full.html.

29 Philip Roth, *American Pastoral* (Boston, MA: Houghton Mifflin Harcourt, 1997).

and closer to our opposites. It attracts us to our opposites so that we can come together with them, side by side, in an embrace of creativity that leads us eventually to wholeness. In literature, art, and life, we are ineluctably attracted to realness, to three-dimensionality, to wholeness. It seems that embedded in every life experience is its opposite, which yearns also to be recognized and expressed.

While none of us is likely to become a famous artist like Shakespeare, he is another good example of how creative work helps us build our puzzle. We could say that the Shakespeare puzzle consists of his collected works. All the parts that are played in Shakespeare are reflections of parts of himself that emerged as he wrote. As he said, "One man in his time plays many parts."[30] The same universal font of words that was available to Shakespeare is available to us all. Even if we can't work his kind of magic, we can engage in the same process and discover the parts of ourselves that belong to our puzzle.

We never totally complete our puzzle. Life is asymptotic. But each step toward completion brings increasing meaning. Our capacity to move ever closer to the endpoint leads to discoveries and developments of enormous value to our society.

This asymptotic gap is actually essential to our creativity. It is in this gap between the last word, the last note, and the last brushstroke that the next word, note, and brushstroke are created. It is in this gap that the last thing that existed and the next thing that comes into existence is created. It is in this gap that we find the creative fingerprints that we ultimately leave behind. Unhappiness and its discontent is the longing that repeatedly leads us to this gap in order to find the creative inspiration that leads to great progress and achievement.

---

30 William Shakespeare, *As You Like It*, 2.7.142, accessed June 7, 2016, http:// shakespeare.mit.edu/asyoulikeit/full.html.

III

TRANSFORMATION: CLEANING OUR PSYCHIC AUGEAN STABLES

In this chapter, we advance the thesis that our psychic shit, the toxic residue of all we think and act and feel, fertilizes our creative garden just as bodily shit, the toxic residue of food, fertilizes our flower gardens. Something thought of as lacking value, not worth a shit, becomes priceless when expressed from the inside to the outside. Both types of gardens carry our creative fingerprints.

When patients first come to therapy, it is not unusual for the word "shit" to appear in their presenting statements. Patients may say, "I've got a lot of shit to deal with," or "I feel like a piece of shit." A more colorful presenting image was, "My life is all fucked up, and I feel like a piece of shit that has been hammered flat."

"Shit" is a powerful word that suggests they're dealing with something they perceive as not only bad, but also worthless. Such comments indicate that the patients are thinking of waste products, what is left over after all the good stuff is gone, after the good stuff has been metabolized. Without being particularly conscious of its meaning at the time it is spoken, when patients use the word "shit," they are often thinking of something worthless that smells bad, looks bad, and is bad. "Not worth a shit" is a mainstay of our vocabulary, and in meaning is a close substitute for the word "worthless." "I don't give a shit" suggests something is not worth caring about. Moreover, when these patients refer to shit, they are not thinking of the waste product our bodies produce. They are thinking of psychic shit, the dark, unacceptable, smelly, ugly residue of thoughts, feelings, memories, and behaviors that has not yet been assimilated and discharged from their minds.

What is true for our bodies is also true for our minds. These psychic residuals, like the bodily ones, become toxic if they are not adequately expelled. We speculate that whoever or whatever created our amazing minds and bodies may have run into the problem all creators or inventors tend to run into. Whoever invented the internal combustion engine and decided it needed gas to run also had to figure out how to exhaust its toxic residual. When the Creator figured out humans needed food and water to run on, a way to discharge the toxic residual, the waste, also had to be determined. Similarly, as psychic life developed and individuals began to process thoughts, feelings, and life experiences, a way was needed to discharge the residual, the toxic waste, of those thoughts, feelings, and experiences. In all these cases, if we don't purge the waste, it becomes dangerous. It has a deleterious effect on the very hosts it initially served positively. It makes no difference whether the food is good for us or bad for us. The waste still has to be discharged. It makes no difference whether the thoughts and feelings were good or bad for us initially; their waste has to be expressed, or it becomes toxic. The colon, the anus, and the urinary tract had to be created, just as exhausts had to be created for engines.

In the case of psychic residuals, we had to devise psychic waste treatment processes analogous to those found in our body, automobiles, and civic waste treatment plants. These analogous psychic waste treatment processes have spiritual and psychological origins. The need to treat potentially toxic psychic residuals must have been an important stimulus to the beginnings of religion and, eventually, psychotherapy. This need probably accounted for the development of cleansing rituals like baptism and bathing rituals found in other religions and cultures, as well as for sacred days of atonement like Yom Kippur.

We also know that what may initially be thought of as shit and worthless becomes extremely valuable when it is expressed, moved from the inside to the outside, into the light, where it becomes fertilizer. It transforms waste products into valuable stimulants to creation and growth. Psychic shit can feed our creativity the way fertilizer feeds our gardens.

Waste removal for all cultures and societies, whether its origin is physical or mental, is a Herculean task. In fact, dung removal was one of the twelve impossible tasks that myth tells us confronted Hercules. The cleaning of the Augean stables by Hercules is a well-known Greek myth that has survived for hundreds, perhaps thousands, of years as it passed through many languages, nations, and cultures.

As the story goes, the goddess Hera, determined to hurt Hercules, caused him to become temporarily insane. In that state, he killed his own wife and children.

When he emerged from his insanity, Hercules felt shocked and guilty for what he'd done. As punishment for his crime, he was sentenced to do twelve seemingly impossible labors. The fifth of these was to clean the Augean stables in one day. This assignment was intended to be both humiliating and impossible, since the livestock were divinely healthy (and immortal) and therefore produced an enormous quantity of dung. The Augean stables had not been cleaned in over thirty years, and over a thousand cattle lived there. However, Hercules succeeded by rerouting the rivers Alpheus and Peneus to wash out the filth. It was, perhaps, a kind of initial model for the later development of sacred washings.

For a myth to endure this long and to resonate across so many cultures, it must contain a meaningful and archetypal message of near universal importance. While the meaning of the story of the cleaning of the Augean stables is subject to many interpretations, a case can be made that it has something to do with the widespread importance of washing and cleansing that is related in some fundamental way to the earlier-mentioned cleansing processes and rituals of baptism, Mikveh, Hindu bathing in the Ganges, Yom Kippur, purgatory, and other purification rituals found in other religions such as the Bahai faith, Islam, and Buddhism. While there is an outer aim of cleaning the body, there is usually a deeper inner spiritual purpose of cleansing us of "sin."

We know from our work with patients that guilt is the only feeling that is palpably experienced by us as indisputable evidence that we have done something "bad," that we have somehow "sinned" and left a deposit of psychic shit. Although some may define sin as breaking only those rules prescribed by religion, our subjective experience in life asserts that that is not so. Intellectually, we may make a distinction between ecclesiastical, secular, and parental rules, but viscerally and emotionally we experience them identically. For example, failure—in relationships, work, or art—makes us feel guilty and ashamed[31] emotionally, the same way we feel when we have "sinned." We feel we are worthless or bad, even though we have violated no divine or moral laws. A lot of our guilt is for violation of highly subjective and sometimes whimsi-

---

31 Without some explanation and clarifying definition, there could be some confusion in our use of the words "shame" and "guilt." We suspect that some therapists would be troubled. Therefore, let us explain our use of "shame" and "guilt." First, we need to comment about the distinction that some will draw between guilt and shame. At the intellectual level, there certainly are distinctions to be made, and the differences are significant. However, the differences at the visceral level are much harder to distinguish. At the gut level, we experience these two as identical.

Briefly, with guilt we are rejected for something we did or did not do; with shame, we are rejected for who we are. Guilt can be explained as "experiencing myself as a bad person because I have done something bad or because I have fantasized about doing something bad." Shame can be explained as meaning "I am bad intrinsically." It is a sense of humiliation in which I am devalued as a person.

We feel guilt at transgressions of commandments and rules imposed on us by various authorities. On the other hand, we feel shame because we fall short of some ideal appearance: we are not tall enough, or slim enough, or we are not pretty enough, or we have a crooked nose.

Guilt feels as though it is a violation of something God said; shame feels as though it is related to something parents said. However, because parents are the child's first images of God, to the child, the two feelings seem to come from the same pool. They get hit with guilt and shame long before they are able to make these fine distinctions. For this reason, it seems to us that the visceral feelings we experience from guilt and shame are identical. We are sometimes suspicious that the fine parsing of the technical and intellectual differences between these two concepts can serve as a defense against experiencing the underlying feeling. There may be highly developed feeling individuals who can make this fine differentiation in feeling for themselves, but we think they are pretty rare. For this reason, we lump guilt and shame together.

cal parental and societal ordinances governing cleanliness, order, appearance, achievement, sex, health, and industry. We more often feel guilty for these garden-variety types of transgressions than we do for murder, stealing, or making graven images, which we are less likely to do. Thus, the psychological experience of guilt is far broader than the religious definition of sin would suggest. While sin in religious terms is transgressing divine law, in psychological terms, it includes offending the ideals that are taught to us by parents and other authorities. We have put "sin" and "bad" in quotes because we know that what is defined as sinful or bad can vary greatly among cultures, religions, and families. Thus, "sin," guilt, and the shit that results from them are the unacceptable stuff of our lives that we try to hide and store out of sight until their fumes make us uncomfortable enough or sick enough to deal with them.

Because "sin" and guilt result from such a wide range of thought, feeling, and behavior, we can step on a guilt turd at any and every turn. It makes us feel dirty, and eventually, we have to clean ourselves as best we can. The ubiquity of sin and guilt and the need to deal with its secular, religious, and psychological aftermath likely led to cleansing processes found in most of the psychotherapy disciplines today. These psychological processes are called catharsis, and their primary aim is to clean our psyches by bringing into the light transgressions that have made us feel guilty and unhappy. Aristotle may have been the first to use catharsis in a psychotherapeutic sense. He defined catharsis as "purging of the spirit of morbid and base ideas or emotions by witnessing the playing out of such emotions or ideas on stage."[32]

While these secular cleansing processes serve a psychological purpose, they are similar to the religious rituals and are likely derived from them. They try to unburden souls, relieve suffering, and transform people who undergo them so that they can live more meaningful and effective lives.

In an earlier chapter, we mentioned the cathartic effect of journaling. Negative emotions like unhappiness, anxiety, disappointment, anger, and guilt, as well as traumatic experiences, create much stress and tension that puts pressure on our minds and emotions. Such pressure

---

32 Aristotle, *The Basic Works of Aristotle*, ed. Richard McKeon (New York: Modern Library, 2001), 1458.

can sicken us if we don't find ways to relieve it. As we noted earlier, journaling serves as a kind of psychic cathartic. In their protective sense, negative emotions like anger and fear can be as essential to our well-being as food. Like food, however, once we have absorbed the good part, the remainder can become toxic and needs to be moved. Journaling serves this purpose. All writing probably does to one degree or another. So do other kinds of creative work. All creative work involves moving thoughts, feelings, and intuitions from the inside of our minds to the outside. We express our shit onto pages, canvasses, and musical scores. What was thought of as ugly and worthless can be transformed into something beautiful and valuable. Aristotle believed that the cathartic effect of creative work like plays and music was achieved simply by seeing and hearing them. But it is likely that both the authors and the authors' audiences gain this therapeutic effect from their creative works. Owing to its psychological and spiritual cleansing effect, we have, therefore, concluded that, at some deep level, purgatory (from which we get the word "purgative"), baptism, and other bathing rituals found in many different religions and cultures are connected to creativity and that both serve a similar healing and transformative purpose.

Dreams also have cathartic, healing, and transformative effects. Dreams bring back to consciousness contents that we have stored in the unconscious. The material may be thoughts, feelings, and behaviors that we have repressed. The repressed material that dreams bring to our conscious attention may have lain there a long time and may be causing psychic pain and disorders. Unconscious guilt, especially, can depress us and even lead us to suicide if it is not brought into the light and dealt with. What shows up in dreams is part of the shit in our psychic stables. It's the smelly stuff we've done in life that we want to keep in the dark. Jungians refer to this dark stuff as our "shadow." It's everything we don't want to be or appear to be. But Jungians also know that in this dark stuff new life is often found. As Jung once said, the shadow is 90% pure gold, if we dig it up and process it.[33]

---

33 This comment was attributed to C.G. Jung by the late C. Toni Frey-Wehrlin, a Jungian analyst in Zürich who helped establish the Zürichberg Clinic.

When one of our patients was decrying all the shit he had to deal with, we tried to comfort him by saying that it is normal for people to have a lot of shit to deal with. We all do. To our surprise, he angrily replied, "That may be true, but I can tell you there is no shit like my shit." Of course, he was right. It is our particular shit, when expressed creatively, that gives it our unique signature. It carries our unique identity and colors all our work. Our shit is an important carrier of our creative fingerprints. Freud knew that kids were the first to come up with the idea of poop as a means of artistic expression. Finger-painting with poop is one of our earliest experiences of the creative urge.

Two dreams of patients we worked with illustrate how the cleansing effect of dreams can bring forth unconscious contents that make us creative.

The first is a woman's dream. She dreamed:

> I have died and am in purgatory. I felt neutral, as if the suffering had ended and I was cleansed of sin.

She spent years writing about this dream in a effort to understand its meaning for her life.

The second is a man's dream. He dreamed:

> I am at Dr. Strickland's house. I am talking with him trying to arrange for my son to meet Angela, who was in New England. I found myself in Dr. Strickland's bathroom in long-handle underwear. I was urinating down my leg inside the long handles. Then, I stepped into a bidet waist deep and furiously tried to wash the urine from my leg. Something about the bidet reminded me of baptism.

The dream kept working on him for several days. He began to journal about the dream and what it meant to him, and suddenly he was overwhelmed by an automatic writing experience that produced the following story:

The Story of the Gold Bidet

And there was discord in all the land. France was locked in a great inner conflict that threatened to tear her asunder. She had become one enormous debating society whose inner quarrels and opposing views were sapping her vitality from within. France could no longer speak with one voice. In effect, she had become a Tower of Babel, separated from herself, floundering in a morass of inaction and indecision. She was adrift without direction or purpose. In the few brief years since the second Great War, there had been constant ministerial crises, and the government had fallen sixteen times. In this period of the nation's life, the collapse of governments had become as familiar, and almost as regular and predictable, as the four seasons or the Metro. Civil war was possible. The Motherland herself was threatened by her own children, whom she had borne and nurtured through all the years of struggle and triumph and victory. France was devouring herself.

While the agonies of inner struggle raged on, there arose in France an ever-increasing countervailing force, which was now giving a new hope that the conflicts might be solved, that inner peace and harmony might return. A towering new political figure had surfaced.

Jean Paul Baptiste had just taken office as the new president of France. At the same time, an event of near equal importance was taking place. As Jean Paul had risen through the ranks of government, he had led the forces which brought about an important change in the locus of political power in France. He had shifted, at first imperceptibly and then with increasing strength, the balance of power from the Ministry of External Affairs to the Ministry of the Interior. For centuries, the Ministry of External Affairs had resided at the geographic center of the government of France and had exerted an enormous, dominating influence on the direction of French life and resources. In contrast, until now, the Ministry of the Interior had enjoyed only a subordinate role as reflected by the physical location of the Interior Ministry. It was considerably more distant than the External Ministry from the geographic center of government. On the day Jean Paul took office, he, as President, ordered a symbolic change which moved the Ministry of the Interior to the building formerly occupied by the Ministry of External Affairs, and vice versa.

These changes reflected the urgent need of this great nation to redirect its energies and resources from the previously dominant external affairs to the now suppliant and demanding internal affairs. The time was ripe for this dramatic rebalancing of French life and priorities. And there was great hope. Recent history had created a profound paradox for France. The problem now besetting her contrasted sharply with the expectations she could otherwise have had at this time of her life. With the help of her allies and friends, France's nemesis, her most hated and threatening enemy, had been utterly devastated and divided. No longer would Germany pose this ancient threat to France's security and peace. Throughout history, these aggressive and warlike Huns had attacked this great jewel of femininity and had devoured her sons and resources by the millions over years of struggle, defeat, and, finally, victory. France could now justifiably expect to enjoy this ultimate victory with its hopeful prospects for peace and prosperity. But, sadly, it was not to be. Those bright expectations were unexpectedly dashed by the dark inner conflicts that surfaced just at the moment of apparent victory and success. For reasons inexplicable to most of France, these conflicting elements, whose energies had for centuries been sublimated and pressed into the service of the external victories and accomplishments of France, could no longer be denied. Just at the zenith of success, when she had reached what otherwise would appear to be the most propitious moment in her history, these long-neglected forces asserted themselves and threatened the nation's life.

France now faced the enemy: it was herself. This was the challenge facing France and Jean Paul Baptiste. Jean took office on his 33rd birthday. He had had a spectacular rise to prominence and power. He was the man for the time. Jean Paul had risen from humble beginnings. He was born in a small village of the Massif Central, that great land mass that is located in and dominates the geographic center of France. When he was very young, before the war, his father moved the family to Paris to find work. His father loved France ardently. He loved Paris. He loved his son. While Jean Paul was still an infant, his doting father spent many days and hours with him walking and bussing through Paris to see the great historical markers, the monuments to France's glory, the museums, and the parks. His father was a walking encyclopedia of France's greatness and history. He generously shared this with his son. Jean Paul remembered, as if it were yesterday, his visits to the Étoile and the Arch of Triumph. He remembered the pride his father expressed when he first described to Jean Paul these monuments, "Look there at the tomb of the unknown soldier, under the Arch of Triumph. Its very simplicity in this grandiose setting makes it impressive, don't you think? And the symbolic flame, which never goes out. Yes, son, it is a magnificent symbol!" His father explained animatedly how the arch symbolized all the great victories of France over her external foes as well as the sacrifices she made in achieving them.

Jean Paul Baptiste was seated this morning in his majestic office overlooking the Place de la Concorde, which lay just across the Seine. The view of the Place de la Concorde reminded him once again this morning of his life's newborn purpose, of his personal destiny to redirect the energies and resources of the nation to bring peace to the internal conflicts despoiling his beloved land. His personal destiny was now entwined and coincident with the historical destiny of France.

As Jean Paul drank in the familiar view from childhood, he knew he had crossed his Rubicon. He had just this morning set in motion a giant step aimed at soon achieving his life's destiny and purpose. The plan was now laid for an event which would bring either salvation to France or a final collapse of government. It would bring another ministerial crisis or the long-hoped-for concord of the conflicting parts.

Unbeknownst to Jean Paul, this planned event was motivated by long-forgotten memories from his childhood, latent and powerful thoughts that today directed the details of his conscious activity. Oedipus had been motivated by forgotten memories of his mother that brought destruction to Greece; Jean Paul was motivated by forgotten memories of his mother which might bring salvation, rather than destruction, to France. Jean Paul Baptiste's father was one of the first Frenchmen killed in the second Great War. After his father's death and the occupation, his mother went to work as a telephone operator at the central exchange, the communications nerve center in Paris. Her superior was a German soldier who was, ironically, a rather nice man. The soldier befriended Jean Paul's mother and provided money, food, and a place to live for her and her son.

Jean Paul's mother was torn by conflicting values. On the one hand, she desperately needed the food, the shelter, and the help of the German. In wartime Paris, this might mean the difference between life and death for her and her son. And satisfying this need, she knew, would likely involve return favors on her part to the German. She had little to give but her body and herself. On the one hand, she liked the German; on the other hand, she valued her integrity, her love of country, the memory of her husband, and the respect of her son. One night, her physical needs and her need for security won out. She had brought the German to her garret apartment after the boy was asleep. The tiny flat had a bedroom for herself, a toilet opening off the hall, a kitchen, and a little alcove where the boy slept. She and the German slipped quietly into her room and were making love. Jean Paul was awakened by the noises and crept to the door of his mother's bedroom to peek through the keyhole. And here begins that long-forgotten memory. He saw the love scene. When the lovemaking was over, his mother got up to go to the bathroom off the hallway. Jean Paul scudded quickly to his alcove. But when his mother closed the bathroom door, he again slipped to the keyhole to observe. He saw her sitting on the bidet. Her face portrayed the very image of revulsion and inner torment, a kind of deep conflict that is spawned by betrayal of one's principles. Slowly, she reached back to the faucets to engage the bidet. The showering spray of water began to do its soothing work. In a moment, he saw his mother's face transformed miraculously from its look of torment to an indescribable look of peace and ecstasy. He had to go in. He turned the handle and opened the door. He walked in and said, "Mamma, why are you washing yourself like that?" She replied, "I am washing away my sins." And the young boy could comprehend in her blissful gaze the enormous transformative power of this thing she straddled like a horse and the power of this washing, as reinforced by its repetition by his mother throughout the years of German occupation.

Jean Paul had two other related, yet contrasting, experiences of washing. The first occurred soon after seeing his mother on the bidet. Jean Paul mashed his finger in his mother's presence and exclaimed, "Shit." His mother reprimanded him and told him that she must wash his mouth out with soap for his own salvation. Yet, somehow, this washing did not create in him the same blissful and peaceful feeling the bidet had seemed to bring his mother.

The second experience was in church. He was baptized. Although his expectations were high, the effect was rather ordinary. Yet, the baptismal font did remind him faintly of that bidet and that cleansing experience he observed his mother having months before. These contrasting experiences of washing now left in the young boy's unconscious mind a powerful impression of baptism: to-wit, that baptism outside the bidet was ersatz, a feeble substitute for the real thing; that the bidet, which in profound truth was the baptismal font par excellence, was without rival in bringing bliss and concord to those who knew and used its mysteries.

These memories, then, were the long-forgotten and buried traces that now welled up to direct the thought and action of Jean Paul Baptiste. These traces now led him toward his moment of destiny. The great event toward which his life had been planned and built was about to begin. He left his office, crossed the Seine and the Place de la Concorde, and proceeded up the Avenue des Champs-Élysées toward the place he had chosen for this event to transpire. Now gathered at the Étoile were the leaders of all the competing factions that had brought inner strife to France—the Communists, the Socialists, the Catholics, the Protestants, the aristocracy, and the bourgeoisie, etc. Each of the major factions assembled in one of the boulevards at the point where the boulevards emptied into the Étoile. Workmen had been busy for weeks, and just overnight had completed the final touches. The Arch of Triumph, that symbol of France's external victories, had been removed to a location of lesser importance. In its place lay a giant, solid-gold bidet, which now stood where the Arch had previously stood in the center of the great circle that formed the Étoile. A huge wooden platform had been built around the bidet with stairs leading up to it. This was to be the new symbol given to France by its new President. It was to form the new center for the life of France. Jean Paul Baptiste was now standing on the wooden platform around the huge bidet high above the gathered crowd. A representative of each of the factions had mounted the platform and stood with him. One by one, Jean Paul baptized each of the representatives in the soothing waters of the giant gold bidet. As he baptized, Jean Paul spoke to the crowd, saying, "I baptize you with water to bring inner peace and joy to the nation. But there is one who comes after me who is mightier than I. He will baptize you with the Holy Spirit and with fire. Awaiting that time, I now consecrate the bidets of France and urge you to do for yourselves as long as ye shall live that which I have done for you this day. And the fox will lie down next to the lamb. And swords will be beaten into plowshares. And your Ministry of the Interior shall take precedence over your Ministry of External Affairs. So shall our race and our name endure, just as it has since before the world was." And there was concord in all the land.[34]

Both of these dreamers became writers and published several books. It is as if the cleansing process of expressing these dreams and writing

---

34 Used by permission.

about them triggered a creative process that continued for the remainder of their lives.

In addition to dreams, fairy tales are also a rich source of information about ourselves, especially if we can look at them analytically and interpret them. They are an ancient form of literature that, from the earliest times, has provided messages and themes that help us grow and develop. If we pay attention, we can see ourselves in them, the sweet and the smelly, and identify some important missing pieces of our puzzle. Very often fairy tales deal with the problem of the opposites that we have been discussing. They are a good source of examples of the need to integrate and reconcile the positive and negative opposites if we are to become whole and our lives are to have depth and meaning. In fairy tales, when we unite with our previously repulsive and unacceptable opposite, we find our prince; we get connected to something big and powerful that makes our life rich and secure. We inherit the kingdom. The fairy tale, *The Frog Prince*, is a good example.

The Frog Prince

A beautiful young princess often played in the garden of her father's palace. Her favorite toy was a colorful ball that she would throw up in the air and try to catch. One day, she threw the ball so high in the air that she couldn't see where it went, until a moment later she heard it fall into a nearby pond with a loud splash. She stood at the edge of the pond peering down into the water and looking for the ball, but she couldn't see it anywhere.

Then, she heard a voice say, "I know where your ball is, and I can bring it to you." She looked around, trying to find the source of the voice, but no one was there. All she could see was an ugly, slimy old frog. Puzzled, she asked the frog if it had said something to her. The frog repeated himself, again promising that he could find her ball and bring it back to her. The princess was shocked that such a disgusting creature would address the daughter of the king. She made a few insulting remarks about the frog's ugly appearance and said she didn't talk to such hideous creatures.

The frog said, "Well, then I guess that's the end of your ball," and began to hop away. But the ball was very important to the princess, and, swallowing her distaste, she apologized to the frog and begged him to bring her ball back to her.

The frog replied, "I'd be happy to, in exchange for one small kiss." Desperate for the return of her favorite toy, the princess reluctantly agreed. The frog dived into the pond and, within a few moments, emerged with the ball and deposited it at her feet.

Muttering a hurried, "Thank you," the princess turned away and again began playing with her ball. The frog called after her, reminding her of the promised kiss. She looked at him, aghast. "Can you actually believe that someone of royal blood would kiss a slimy little frog? You must be very naïve." Anxious to end this line of conversation, the princess picked up her ball and returned to the palace.

That night, as the family was gathered around the dinner table, a servant announced to the king that a frog was at the door and wanted to see him.

"Tell him to go away!" the princess said.

"A frog?" asked the king. "What does a frog want?"

The servant said, "He said something about a broken promise, Your Majesty."

"Send him in," said the king. The king listened patiently to the frog's story and then turned to the princess. "Did you promise this frog a kiss in exchange for retrieving your ball?" the king asked.

"Well, yes," she replied, "but surely you can't expect me to kiss something green, slimy, and covered with warts."

"I want you to keep your promise," said the king. "And this frog will remain here until you do."

The princess turned up her nose at the thought and quietly finished her dinner. She excused herself and headed upstairs to her room, with the frog hopping along just a few feet behind her. She sat down in a nearby chair to read, and when she looked up, she found the frog perched on the arm of the chair, staring up at her. Finally, she headed to bed, and the frog jumped up onto her pillow and fell asleep beside her.

Several days passed in this fashion. Eventually, the princess found that the frog was a fine playmate. She'd throw her ball into the air, and the frog would hop after it and bring it back. She would read her favorite books aloud, and they'd laugh together at the funniest passages. And each night, the frog would sleep beside her on her pillow. One night, as she was drifting off to sleep, the princess looked over at the frog and, almost without thinking, said "Good night," and leaned over and gave him a kiss.

Suddenly, the frog disappeared, and, in his place appeared a handsome prince. He told the princess about an evil fairy who had cursed him, turned him into a frog, and told him he would remain so until the day a princess should give him a kiss. Of course, the princess was overjoyed. Since the two of them had already become the best of friends, they soon married, and, naturally, lived happily ever after.

Fairy tales like *The Frog Prince* that have long been passed from one generation to the next have stressed the indispensable importance of the negative in our lives. We love reading this story about the importance of the negatives; we hate practicing it. They tell us we have to kiss the frog or, as in *Beauty and the Beast*, embrace the ugly beast, if we are to find our prince, if we are to be saved from a dull, ordinary, insecure, and meaningless life. We have to link up with something powerful and supportive that will protect us and help us thrive by completing the meaning of our lives.

Creativity and Guilt

The relationship between creativity and guilt is complicated. It is complicated because guilt both inhibits and fosters creativity.

On the one hand, guilt is a guardian of conventional values. As such, it tends to inhibit creative change by supporting the status quo, the currently acceptable way. We feel guilty not only when we trespass divine ordinances but also secular laws and conventional rules and tastes. The more creative we are, the more we tend to challenge these laws, rules, and tastes. Creativity implies change and usually involves something new. The new thing may be conventionally acceptable, but it often is not. Galileo's creative insight that the sun, not the earth, is the center of the universe not only violated conventional beliefs but also the views of the church. He nearly got burned at the stake. Only by renouncing his new idea could he save himself. The church didn't accept the new idea for two hundred more years. And then there are new schools of art, like the impressionists, who ran into huge roadblocks from the cultural establishment that discouraged their work. Only the persistence and courage of the artists permitted the world to benefit from this new creative wave. Examples of the interference of guilt with creativity are legion. We can think of Darwin and the huge guilt he incurred for his new ideas about evolution.

On the other hand, guilt paradoxically plays a huge role in fostering creativity. In this way, guilt contradicts itself. That may be why some of our greatest art contains internal contradictions of its own. For example, in a review of a Cézanne exhibit, the writer remarked that, "the opposing principles of conformity and rebellion also inform almost every picture he painted. That's one reason his paintings are so unfathomably great: A single Cézanne canvas can assert both one thing and its exact opposite. As your reading of the painting shifts, it can become its antithesis…. As I hope I have shown by now, fascinated frustration and frustrated fascination are what Cézanne is all about."[35] Similarly, all great literature contains contradictions. Dr. Jekyll and Mr. Hyde is but one of many well-known examples.

The contradiction in guilt's tendency to inhibit creativity can be seen in its equally strong proclivity to foster it. Guilt fosters creativity by making us unhappy. As we saw in the first chapter, unhappiness goads us into creative activity. We create because we believe it will relieve our unhappiness. While there are many causes of unhappiness that can disturb our equilibrium, guilt-induced unhappiness is the most powerful. We may feel very unhappy because our dress didn't get back

---

35 Blake Gopnik, "Sublimely at Odds," *Washington Post* (Washington, DC), Jan. 29, 2006, sec. N, p. 1, 6.

from the cleaners in time for the dance. Or someone may have slighted us. Or we didn't get a promotion. This unhappiness can be quite painful. Generally, however, this form of unhappiness doesn't put us at risk. We can bear those painful feelings more easily and with less threat to our selves and our lives than we can bear the unhappiness caused by feelings of guilt, especially unconscious guilt. Guilt is the only feeling that we palpably experience as indisputable evidence that we are "bad." At some deep level we feel we have failed God. Thus, while unhappiness from other causes is painful and menacing enough, this unhappiness does not hit our vital spots; it attacks our walls. Guilt-based unhappiness, on the other hand, assaults our foundation, our sense of self-worth. Thus, in guilt-based unhappiness, we create not only to relieve our unhappiness but also to redeem ourselves, in order to restore our worth.

In the end, we believe it is unconscious unhappiness and the unconscious guilt that lies behind it that is a major and essential source of creative energy and production. The feeling works on us in the dark and drives us to create things that will close the gap that represents the shortfall in our lives that makes us feel unworthy. The gap we attempt to close with our creative efforts is that space between naked reality, the way things actually are, and our cherished ideals, the way we wish things could be and feel they ought to be. This gap is painful, because we feel it represents and reflects our personal failure to live up to our potential. The result of this personal failure is a profound feeling of guilt.

Closing the gap is the work of redemption. We redeem ourselves by discovering and expressing in what we create rejected unconscious parts of ourselves. But, as we have pointed out, guilt is contradictory. The more creative we become, the more at odds we are with conventional and ecclesiastical society, and the more guilt we feel. The creative person atones for his guilt by giving back to the collective the products of his creative work, just as Prometheus did. Jungians might say that there is an inner unconscious archetypal pressure that leads us to expiate in this way.

Thus, the cycle of creation, guilt, and redemption repeats itself. If it didn't repeat itself, creation would end. Guilt is essential not only to sparking creation, but also to maintaining it. Creation is atonement, and we have to atone again and again if we are to hold onto our self-worth and, perhaps, our lives.

This inner pressure to create, and the need for redemption from the guilt it induces, flow from a common source. They originate in the conflict of opposites, between two different thoughts, actions, and feelings, one of which is conscious and the other unconscious. As discussed earlier, the opposites are fundamental to all creation, wherever it occurs. They are our cosmic parents who come together to create life in all its forms. Physical intercourse between masculine and feminine opposites creates a child. Psychic intercourse between our masculine and feminine psychological opposites also produces a "child," but in another form. Creative production resolves the conflict between them at least momentarily. It is in this moment, when the warring opposites are resolved, when the male and the female unite, that something new is born. The "baby" produced by this union may be an infant or a work of art. Both release momentarily the tension that existed between the opposites. There is the physical moment of orgasm or the "aha" moment of creative insight. The creative moment both produces something new and redeems guilt. Redemption by the birth of something new is fundamental to the Christian story of salvation.

The moment of creativity releases us from guilt. It releases us because, in order to create, we have to unite polar opposites. The union of opposites that is a prerequisite to creativity produces an "at-one-ment," an atonement. That's why we experience the feeling of redemption when we create. But the moment after, we begin to feel guilt again. Because the opposites are a precondition to creativity, they must reform after each creative act that resolved them. We spend our lives embracing the opposites and then pushing them away in a creative dance that sustains life.

Each new step in creation incurs guilt that must be followed by another step in creation and redemption. It is an endless developmental cycle, filled both with suffering and reward for suffering, which together keep building our world until we die. The attainment of permanent redemption while we are alive would mean the end of creation. That may be why purgatory is conceived as an afterlife experience, when remaining guilt and sin are purged and absolved.

We believe that fundamentally it is guilt that lies behind our unhappiness, our Divine Discontent, and that it is the need to rid ourselves of guilt and its pain that leads us to the constant striving and work that creates our selves and our world. This may be why Jung wrote unqualifiedly that "life itself is guilt."[36] Since we all must, in order to live, experience guilt and the pain it inflicts, our stories and our creative work are somehow, at some deep level, about redemption. In this deep way, we become connected to each other and to each other's work.

Fundamentally, our stories and our creative work redeem what was rejected. As the Bible reminds us, "the stone which the builders rejected, the same is become the head of the corner."[37] It becomes the cornerstone, the stone that joins the opposite sides of a building and locks the stones in place. It is the stone on which the other interrelated stones depend. It's the place from which our creativity and our being started. And we remain uniquely connected to it and obstinately reflect it in the recurrent themes of our work.

We believe that guilt, painful as it is, may be the Self's gift to humanity, just as fire was Prometheus' gift. We imagine that the Self devised guilt not primarily to make us "good," important as that purpose may be, but to be a critical catalyst for the creative energy necessary to build our world and ourselves. We can also believe that the Self introduced guilt in order to make creators of us all and thereby draw us closer to the Self. As Augustine put it, "Thou madest us for Thyself, and our heart is restless until it repose in Thee."[38] Thus, the ultimate aim of Divine Discontent and the creativity it fosters is ever-higher stages of artistic and cultural achievement whose endpoint is the realm of the Divine and an ever-closer connection with the Creator who dwells there.

---

36 C.G. Jung, 1970. "The Personification of the Opposites," CW 14, ¶ 206.

37 Matthew 21:42 (King James Version).

38 Augustine of Hippo, "The Confessions of Saint Augustine," *Internet Sacred Text Archive*, 2011, http://www.sacred-texts.com/chr/augconf/aug01.htm.

IV

CREATIVITY AND REBIRTH

Everyone in his time has many birthdays. The first one, of course, is our actual birth day, the day on which we are physically born. We are more familiar with this one. We usually celebrate it or recognize it in some fashion. What we may not be so aware of, recognize, give voice to, or celebrate is the subsequent births that are psychological rather than physical in nature. These may be our more important birthdays. In our first birth, we are born to our parents and into their world and belief systems, which shape the way we think, act, and feel. Subsequent births are psychological births in which we are born increasingly to ourselves rather than to our parents. These births are the result of an inner psychological intercourse of masculine and feminine opposites in which we become our own parents, giving birth to ourselves.

We are born again at each pivotal moment in our lives when some important change gives birth to a new way of thinking, acting, or feeling that is different from the default ways that were shaped primarily by our parents. We may know these pivotal moments at the instant they happen. Often, however, we may become aware of them only in retrospect, when distance from them provides the perspective necessary to see them and to grasp for the first time their meaning and the transformative significance they have had on our lives.

For example, sometimes a doctor, lawyer, or artist can tell you the moment early in his life that he knew he wanted to become what he eventually became. Recovering addicts often remember the exact time and circumstance when the resolve and the strength to stop using came to them. Many members of Alcoholics Anonymous think of the day they stopped drinking as their second birthday, their real birthday, which they celebrate annually just as they do their physical birth. While it may take years for all of the changes connected to the second birth experience to manifest in our lives, the inner changes that must precede the outer changes often transpire in a matter of seconds.

A death precedes all new births. We have to let go of old ways of thinking, acting, and feeling before the new can enter our lives. Both the death and the birth can seem to happen simultaneously. The wish, and often the struggle, to let go of some old way of thinking or living may go on for years before the death actually occurs and new life can emerge.

The determined wish to fully be ourselves cannot be satisfied until our selves are fully born. Only then will we be true to ourselves. Our truth grows into greater fullness as our selves grow into greater fullness. Each moment of significant change in our lives is a birth that adds to the cumulative experience of self.

Many religions have powerful rituals and symbols that express their beliefs in rebirth. Baptism is, perhaps, the best known of these, at least in the Christian world. Death and rebirth are among the most important meanings of baptism. Baptism signifies the death of sin, which is achieved by washing it away, and the birth of the Christian. Pope Francis emphasized the importance of this second birthday to Catholics and urged them celebrate it to commemorate the act of birth into the church just as faithfully and fully as they celebrate their physical birth. Catholics are given a new name, their Christian name, at the completion of this rebirth ritual.[39]

Most of the important birth experiences we have in life subsequent to our physical birth, however, are not connected to any sect or religion. They are personal. They are direct. They are powerful. There is no congregation to witness them. They are not observed collectively. They happen when we are alone, as we observe ourselves experiencing ourselves. These experiences are inner experiences that are associated

---

39 Vatican Information Service, *Pope Francis: Find Out the Date of Your Baptism and Celebrate It!* (London: Independent Catholic News, 2014), http://www.indcatholicnews.com/news.php?viewStory=23921.

with a palpably deep feeling that changed us, that somehow altered the course of our lives. Often the experience comes after a long period of suffering during which we were unable to change through our own will or intention. It feels much more like something that happened to us than something we made happen.

The feeling may sweep over us or come to us more quietly. We remember one of these quiet experiences as reported by one of our patients. He was a recovering alcoholic. He had drunk heavily for years. He had frequent blackouts in which he often did outrageous things that he only knew about because someone told him what he had done while he was heavily intoxicated. He lost his job. His marriage failed. He was in an auto wreck and hurt badly. He lived with terrible guilt but simply could not find the will or the strength to stop. One morning after years of struggle, he woke up from a painful hangover and from a blackout. He had no memory of what he had done since about four o'clock the previous afternoon. He didn't remember where his car was. He was too sick to go to work at a new job that he had miraculously gotten with the help of a friend. He was sitting alone feeling depressed, guilty, and afraid. To himself, he simply said, "God help me." At that very moment, he felt a burden lift. A feeling of resolve came to him. This resolve led him to call Alcoholics Anonymous and go to a meeting. He never drank again after that moment. While it took a few years for the effect of this inner change to appear in his life, he eventually became a very successful businessman and continued to help other alcoholics.

Although these death and rebirth experiences usually do not happen in church, they nevertheless have a religious feeling and quality about them. They feel sacred and special to us when we have them. We never forget them. The experience feels as sacred as a collective religious experience like baptism, if not more so. While the experiences we are referring to resemble in certain ways those that William James describes in his classic book, *The Varieties of Religious Experience*, the experiences we are describing are not associated with any formal religion or institution. Nor do they involve visions of deities. Rather, they are intensely personal and individual.

Artists know the moment of this experience as the creative moment, the "aha" moment when a new creative insight is born. But most people, not just artists, have these so-called "aha" moments in their lives, although some have the experience more often than others. We can wonder why people with such diverse backgrounds and experiences can have these moments of insight and change that seem so identical at the feeling level.

The results in outer life of this seemingly identical inner moment may vary widely. It may involve being freed of an addiction or abandoning an abusive relationship, or it may inspire a career change or lead to the idea for a novel, painting, or symphony. But inside, the experience feels the same. Since something old dies and something new is born in all these cases, one can sense that somehow, despite all the outer differences, some similar inner connection has been made to a creative source with the power to transform.

In most of life, creation occurs only when polar opposites—masculine and feminine, positive and negative—unite. As we notice with electricity, the current begins to flow and the light goes on only when the positive and negative opposite poles connect.

When the opposites unite, something new is born. A child is born. A light is born. A book is born. A new insight, a new idea, or, perhaps, a new attitude arrives. Usually it is unexpected. There is a continuous dance of these opposites in our lives. They dance separately and then momentarily come together to form a new entity, one that is neither of its parts but somehow contains them both, just as a newborn child is neither its mother or its father, yet contains them both. This dance gives birth continuously to something new. It's an interior dance that occurs inside of us, in our psyches.

It is this self that is born within that we so unshakably want to be. We experience this desire as the urge to be true to ourselves. And these births *are* true to ourselves, because they are a direct experience. We did not receive them from the outside or from any other source. Many of the experiences we have in our religious faiths as Christians, Muslims, or Buddhists are indirect in this sense. In turn, many of the religious beliefs, rituals, practices, doctrines, and behaviors of these faiths come from the direct experiences of religious figures such as Christ, Muhammad, Moses, or the Buddha. In this way, our psychic rebirths may actually distance us from the beliefs and practices in our lives that had been shaped by our religions. Being true to ourselves can be very different from being true to our traditional religious faiths or to any other system of belief or conventional standard.

The drive and the determination to be true to ourselves, to live by our direct experience rather than someone else's, is captured brilliantly in the Netflix television series called *Chef's Table*. It's the story of sixteen world-renowned chefs who are creative artists in their own right.

Great chefs count among the great artists of the world. Their enormous creativity manifests itself not only in the flavors, colors, and textures of the food they prepare but also in its presentation. The décor of their restaurants, their tables, and the ambiance they create are often artistic masterpieces, which they then integrate into a wondrous artistic whole. They often express great courage in breaking with conventionally accepted and established gastronomy.

When we read the biographies of these creative masters, we see an insistent urge not only to create and to change, but also to be true to themselves. As such, they are often examples of life influenced by direct experience. They have inner experiences that not only lead them to their careers but also to insights that produce cuisine that is true to them but at variance with currently accepted standards of fine dining. For example, in some circles cooking the French way is the dominant gastronomic ethic, and in such milieus, French cuisine may be the only thing considered truly "fine." To vary from this standard is considered gastronomic apostasy. Nonetheless, these great creative chefs often offer something quite different. Their deviation from the gastronomic ethic would be analogous to varying from the Christian path in a society dominated by Christianity. Being a non-conformist is risky, whether it is in cooking or religious belief.

The Christian lives an indirect experience that conforms to the beliefs and paths developed by another, while the apostate lives a direct experience based on his own beliefs, beliefs that grew from within. There is much more risk in the heathen's way, but it may be the only way by which big changes are brought about.

One of the *Chef's Table* vignettes is about Alex Atala, a Brazilian chef whose restaurant, D.O.M., is ranked as the ninth best restaurant in the world by the San Pellegrino guide to the world's fifty best restaurants. The story of Alex in this television series noted that "when he was growing up in São Paulo, eating out meant going to a French or Italian restaurant. They were the only important ones. And French chefs were the gods in Brazil. Going to a good restaurant was something for the wealthy. Brazilians did not think of their cuisine as restaurant food, as cuisine that has great gastronomic value, a cuisine worthy of the ritual of dressing up, getting ready, and going out to eat."

So, Alex trained in France and worked there and in Italy for several years before returning to Brazil. He had mastered French cooking techniques and began working in a French restaurant in São Paulo. At some point, the French chef told Alex that he would never make a French dinner as good as the French chef's dinners were. It hurt, but then Alex had one of those moments of clarity and insight, which created a turning point in his life. He looked in the mirror, saw his tattoos and his face, and said to himself, "You are a Brazilian man. You are an outsider. If I'm not able to make a French dinner as good as a French chef, nobody could make a Brazilian dinner and experience as good as me."

"I was allowed to cook some Brazilian dishes and began to switch ingredients. I took flounder and served it with a passion fruit *farofa*. People loved it. This was my moment. I decided to open my own restaurant. I decided to cook things that came from deep in my heart. A Brazilian cuisine worth dressing up for and going out. I drew heavily on ingredients from the Amazon region. But I don't think all chefs need to go to the jungle and the river. This was my truth. My way." For Alex, this was a kind of personal diaspora. He left himself and went to France, where he imitated others. Then he came home to Brazil, found himself again, and expressed it.

Another wonderful story of finding one's self is about Magnus Nilsson, whose restaurant, Fäviken, is ranked nineteenth on the San Pellegrino list of the world's fifty great restaurants. The restaurant is in

Järpen, Sweden, a small community of less than 1,500 people. It is a fine dining restaurant in the middle of nowhere. As Magnus says, "Up here there is only us." The restaurant seats twelve people who come from around the world to eat the thirty-course tasting menu served at this remote place.

After attending cooking school in Sweden, Magnus decided to go to Paris, a place he thought would make him a better chef. As a food critic noted, "You go to France to be trained in cooking. There's a tradition of it and it's brutal and brilliant. It doesn't mean you'll be creative or come up with new recipes or even be successful. But you have tools you can't get anywhere else." Magnus worked in fine French restaurants for several years.

At some point he returned to Stockholm and worked as a chef in a restaurant there. Like Alex, Magnus had a pivotal moment that changed his life and shaped his future. In the restaurant in Stockholm he began to feel everything he was doing was colored by his French experience. It wasn't his. "It just felt like less well-executed copies of someone else's stuff. It turned me off from cooking completely. I didn't want to go back in the kitchen." That's what happens when the "not I" crowds out the "I." We can feel that whatever we are thinking, feeling, or doing some-how doesn't fit the great puzzle that is us. Our work no longer resonates with our selves.

He left and returned home. There, the owners of the Fäviken restau-rant asked him to consult with them and help them make something of their small restaurant. As he began to think about the kind of restaurant that would reflect him, he finally got back in the kitchen, because there was no one else who could do it. As one food critic put it, "He stripped away all the trappings of classical Michelin-starred fancy cuisine. He's doing things exactly his way and no other way. It's a kind of magical circle he has completed. Not just by realizing there are all these local ingredients he can work with, but he's kind of come home. He's become Magnus the Viking."

Both Magnus and Alex experienced this kind of diaspora. The "not I" in their lives led to much suffering, but they eventually were healed when they were reborn to themselves.

All of these great chefs have many qualities in common. One of the most important is an inner urge to be true to themselves. As award-winning chef Niki Nakayama noted, "I came to believe that I deserved to open a restaurant that I 100 percent believed was who I am. People can sense who I am when they eat my food." While she doesn't leave her physical fingerprint on her food, she does leave a creative fingerprint on it, a telltale mark that reflects her unique self.

At our first birth, we have physical fingerprints, small and faint as they may be, that identify us. It is in our subsequent births that we grow and develop this other creative fingerprint. This creative print appears in our work and grows deeper and richer. If we are lucky, our creative work and experiences develop them to a full-bodied clarity. Over their careers Niki Nakayama, as well as most of the artists featured in *Chef's Table*, develop this clarity that is seen and known by them and others.

If we want to develop our creative fingerprint as fully and clearly as these artist chefs, we, like them, have to be as true as we possibly can to ourselves. To be true to ourselves, we first have to know ourselves. We, like them, have to observe our thoughts, feelings, and actions, reflect on them and take the insights that come from them seriously enough to express them in our lives. Only by bearing witness to ourselves can we become ourselves. And, like them, we are likely to be most true to ourselves and to express that truth when we are doing the creative work we come to believe we were meant to do.

AFTERWORD

One evening after we had finished writing *Our Creative Fingerprint*, we stumbled upon a Netflix original movie called *Tallulah*.[40] We were very pleasantly surprised when a powerful scene took place that seemed to us to capture the essence of what our book is about. In this scene, a woman writer, Margo, is talking with a friend, who is seated on the floor surrounded by several paintings that had belonged to Margo's husband. Margo inadvertently knocks over an open can of paint, a large glob of which lands squarely on one of the paintings. She bursts out angrily at her friend for putting the paintings and the can of paint on the floor in the first place. Then, looking at her friend, Margo is reminded that, earlier that day, she had said she hated her husband's paintings but couldn't get rid of them because they didn't belong to her.

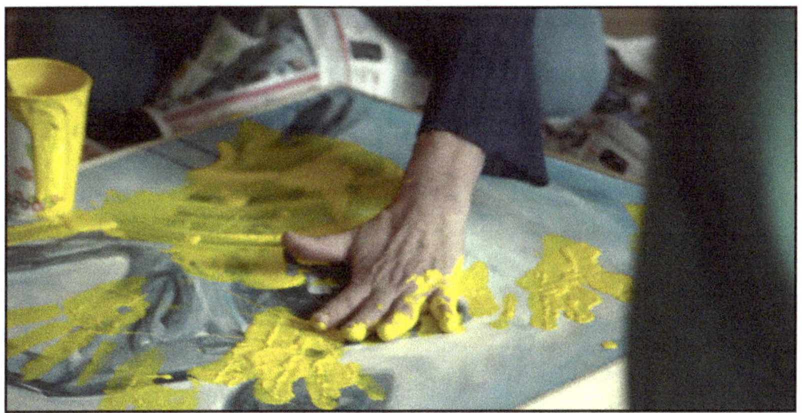

Figure 7: In a scene from the film, *Tallulah*, a writer, Margo, stamps her handprint in yellow paint all over one of her husband's paintings. (Reprinted with permission from Route One Entertainment.)

Margo considers this for a moment, then puts her fingers in the glob of spilled yellow paint and begins to smear her fingerprints all over her husband's painting. She looks over at her friend, who says, "Now, it is yours."

---

40 *Tallulah*, directed by Sian Heder (2016; Beverly Hills, CA: Mother Pictures, LLC, 2016), https://www.netflix.com/title/80098201

REFERENCES

A Civil Action. Directed by Steven Zaillian. 1998. Burbank, CA: Touchstone Pictures, 1999. DVD.

Augustine of Hippo. "The Confessions of Saint Augustine." *Internet Sacred Text Archive.* 2011. http://www.sacred-texts.com/chr/augconf/aug01.htm.

Aristotle. *The Basic Works of Aristotle,* Edited by Richard McKeon. New York: Modern Library, 2001.

Cartwright, Mark. "Aztec Sacrifice." *Ancient History Encyclopedia.* September 2, 2013. http://www.ancient.eu/Aztec_Sacrifice/.

Crash. Directed by Paul Haggis. 2004. Santa Monica, CA: Lionsgate Films, 2005. DVD.

Frida. Directed by Julie Taymor. 2002. Santa Monica, CA: Miramax Lionsgate, 2003. DVD.

Gopnik, Blake. "Sublimely at Odds." *Washington Post* (Washington, DC), Jan. 29, 2006.

High Strung. Directed by Michael Damian. 2016. Leeds, UK: Riviera Films, LLC, and High Strung, LLC, 2016. https://www.netflix.com/title/80098201.

Jung, C.G. *The Collected Works, Second Edition.* (Bollingen Series XX; H. Read, M. Fordham, & G. Adler, Eds.; R. F. C. Hull, Trans.). Princeton, NJ: Princeton University Press, 1953-1979.

— *On the Psychology of the Trickster-Figure, The Collected Works Vol. 9i, Second Edition.* (Bollingen Series XX). Princeton, NJ: Princeton University Press, 1969.

— *Psychological Aspects of the Mother Archetype, The Collected Works Vol. 9i, Second Edition.* (Bollingen Series XX). Princeton, NJ: Princeton University Press, 1969.

— *The Ego, The Collected Works Vol. 9ii, Second Edition.* (Bollingen Series XX). Princeton, NJ: Princeton University Press, 1969.

— *The Mana-Personality, The Collected Works Vol. 7, Second Edition.* (Bollingen Series XX). Princeton, NJ: Princeton University Press, 1967.

— *The Personification of the Opposites, The Collected Works Vol. 14, Second Edition.* (Bollingen Series XX). Princeton, NJ: Princeton University Press, 1970.

— *The Problem of the Attitude Type, The Collected Works Vol. 7, Second Edition.* (Bollingen Series XX). Princeton, NJ: Princeton University Press, 1967.

— *The Psychology of the Child Archetype, The Collected Works Vol. 9i, Second Edition.* (Bollingen Series XX). Princeton, NJ: Princeton University Press, 1969.

Lawrence of Arabia. Directed by David Lean. 1962. UK: Horizon Pictures, 2001. DVD.

Like Water for Chocolate. Directed by Alfonso Arau. 1993. Santa Monica, CA: Miramax Lionsgate, 2000. DVD.

Martin, Philip. *Wallander,* "Sidetracked." TV Series. Directed by Philip Martin. 2008. London, UK: BBC Video, 2009. DVD.

Prignitz-Poda, Helga. *Frida Kahlo: The Painter and Her Work.* Munich: Schirmer/Mosel Publishers, 2004.

Puccini, Giacomo. *Tosca.* Milan, Italy: Giulio Ricordi & Co., 1895.

Robinson, Edwin Arlington. "Richard Cory." *The Poetry Foundation.* 1897. http://www.poetryfoundation.org/poems-and-poets/poems/detail/44982.

Roth, Philip. *American Pastoral.* Boston, MA: Houghton Mifflin Harcourt, 1997.

Shakespeare, William. "As You Like It." *Massachusetts Institute of Technology.* Accessed June 7, 2016. http://shakespeare.mit.edu/asyoulikeit/full.html.

Shakespeare, William. "The Tragedy of Hamlet, Prince of Denmark." *Massachusetts Institute of Technology.* Accessed June 8, 2016. http://shakespeare.mit.edu/hamlet/full.html.

Tallulah. Directed by Sian Heder. 2016. Beverly Hills, CA: Mother Pictures, LLC, 2016. https://www.netflix.com/title/80093198.

van Druten, John. *I Am A Camera: A Play in Three Acts.* New York: Dramatists Play Service, 1983. http://www.worldcat.org/title/i-am-a-camera-a-play-in-three-acts/oclc/879155434/viewport.

Vatican Information Service. *Pope Francis: Find Out the Date of Your Baptism and Celebrate It!* London: Independent Catholic News, 2014. http://www.indcatholicnews.com/news.php?viewStory=23921.

INDEX

A

abusive relationship 70
abusive relationship, abandoning an
      70
A Civil Action (movie) 44, 45, 76
addiction, freed of an 70
addiction(s) 27, 70
Aeneas 20
"aha" moment 65, 70
Alcoholics Anonymous 68, 69
American Pastoral (movie) 45, 77
anger 26, 51, 52
anxiety 33, 34, 51
Aristotle 51, 52, 76
asymptotic 26, 27, 46
asymptotic gap 46
atonement 48, 64, 65
Augean stables 49
Augustine 66, 76
autonomic nervous system 5

B

Bahai faith 49
baptism 48, 49, 52, 53, 58, 68, 69
bathing 48, 49, 52
bathing in the Ganges 49
Beauty and the Beast (play) 62
Beethoven 1
Buddhism 49

C

Caravaggio 1
Carnegie, Andrew 29

catharsis 51
cathartic effect 32, 51, 52
Cézanne, Paul 4, 63
Chac Mool 10
Chartres 39
Chef's Table (television series) 71,
      72, 74
Churchill, Winston 37
cleaning of the Augean stables 49
cleansing effect of dreams 53
cleansing process 49, 51, 59
content 27, 42
conventional rules 62
Cory, Richard 30, 77
Crash (movie) 44, 45, 76
creative activity 23, 40, 63
creative fingerprint(s) 74
creative inspiration 4, 46
creative process vii, 8, 43, 60
creative urge 53
creative work 1, 2, 4, 5, 6, 8, 22, 43,
      46, 52, 64, 66, 74
creativity and guilt 62

D

Darwin, Charles 29, 63
death and rebirth 68
Declaration of Independence 24
developmental cycle 65
Dido 20
disappointment 26, 51
discontent 23, 24, 26, 27, 46
Divine Discontent 23, 25, 27, 41,
      66

E

ego-weakening tendency 6
Einstein, Albert 1
embrace the ugly beast 62

F

failed marriage 69
fear 44, 52
fertilizer 48, 49
finger-painting 53
fingerprints 1, 2, 23, 46, 47, 53, 74
Freud, Sigmund 6, 7, 53
fulfillment 22, 41

G

Galileo 63
giving birth to ourselves 67
Goethe, Johann Wolfgang 12, 23, 24
  "Ginkgo Biloba" 12
guilt 8, 26, 29, 31, 34, 49, 50, 51,
    52, 62, 63, 64, 65, 66, 69
guilt-induced unhappiness 63

H

Hamlet (play) 45, 77
happiness 23, 24, 25, 27, 28, 39, 40
harsh judgment 2
Hemingway, Ernest 1, 29, 30
Hera 49
Hercules 49
High Strung (movie) 35, 76
Homer, Winslow 3, 4

I

inner guidance system 32
Islam 49

J

James, William 69

The Varieties of Religious Experience
    69
Jekyll and Hyde 45, 63
journaling 31, 32, 40, 51, 52

K

Kahlo, Frida 4, 8, 9, 10, 11, 13, 15,
    17, 18, 19, 20, 21, 77
  Me and My Parrots 14, 15
  *Self Portrait as a Tehuana or Diego in
    My Thoughts* 16
  The Broken Column 18, 19
  The Two Fridas 12, 13
  The Wounded Deer 20, 21
  What I Saw in the Water 9, 11
Kahn, Louis 1

L

Lawrence of Arabia (movie) 44, 45,
    77
Like Water for Chocolate (movie) 8,
    77

M

Mad Men (television series) 25
Manet, Édouard 1
masculine and feminine opposites
    44, 65, 67
meditation 4, 43
Modiano, Patrick 3

N

narcissistic self-absorption 31
negative animus 10
non-conformist 71

O

opposites unite 70

P

Picasso, Pablo 1
Pope Francis 68, 77
positive and negative opposites 60
powerless 32, 33, 34
powerlessness 33, 34, 35
prayer 43
Prignitz-Poda, Helga 8, 9, 10, 18, 20, 77
Prometheus 64, 66
psychic bowel movement 32
psychic intercourse 65
psychic residuals 48
psychic waste treatment processes 48
psychological birth(s) 67
psychological opposites 65
psychological suffering 18
punishment for crime 49
purgatory 49, 52, 53, 66
puritanical 8
puzzle 31, 38, 39, 40, 41, 42, 43, 46, 60, 73

R

rebirth 68, 69
recurring leitmotifs 2
redemption 20, 64, 65, 66
religious rituals 51
Rivera, Diego 10, 11, 13, 15, 17, 19, 21
roten faden 2
Roth, Philip 45, 77

S

second birth 68
secular laws 62
self-discovery 4, 6, 8
self-portraits 2, 4, 9
self-portraiture 2
self-worth 64, 65

Shakespeare, William ix, 45, 46, 77
sin and guilt 51
Skinner, B.F. 26
Stravinsky, Igor 1
suffering 18, 20, 28, 29, 30, 51, 53, 65, 73, 74
suicide 20, 52

T

Tallulah (film) iv, 75, 75
Tennyson, Alfred (Lord) 4
The Frog Prince (fairy tale) 60, 62
Tosca (opera) 45, 77
toxic residual 48
toxic waste 48
traumatic experiences 51

U

unconscious guilt 52, 64
unconscious reservoir 4
unconscious unhappiness 64
unhappiness vii, viii, 23, 24, 25, 27, 28, 29, 30, 31, 32, 35, 38, 39, 40, 43, 46, 51, 63, 64, 66
union of opposites 65

V

Vivaldi, Antonio 3, 4

W

Wagner, Richard 1
washing and cleansing 49
wholeness 9, 14, 20, 22, 39, 40, 41, 46
World War II 37, 38
Wright, Frank Lloyd 1

Y

Yom Kippur 48, 49

Also by

Nancy Carter Pennington and Lawrence H. Staples

Guilt with a Twist: The Promethean Way
ISBN 978-0-9776076-4-8

The Creative Soul: Art and the Quest for Wholeness
ISBN 978-0-9810344-4-7

The Guilt Cure
ISBN 978-1-926715-53-7